W9-AUO-514

MARCO POLO

PORTUGAL

with Local Tips

*The author's special recommendations are
highlighted in yellow throughout this guide*

There are five symbols to help you find your way around this guide:

★

Marco Polo's top recommendations – the best in each category

sites with a scenic view

places where the local people meet

places where young people get together

(100/A1)
pages and coordinates for the Road Atlas of Portugal
(U/A1) *coordinates for the City Map of Lisbon inside back cover*
(O) *area not covered by the City Map of Lisbon*

*This guide was written by Alois Weimer and Britta Weimer-Langer.
Alois Weimer taught for seven years in the German School in Oporto
and at the University in Braga. His daughter Britta grew up in Portugal
and studied in Lisbon.*

MARCO ⊕ POLO

Travel guides and language guides in this series:

Alaska • Algarve • Amsterdam • Australia/Sydney • Bahamas • Barbados
Barcelona • Berlin • Brittany • Brussels • California • Canada • Channel
Islands • Chicago and the Great Lakes • Costa Brava/Barcelona • Costa del
Sol/Granada • Côte d'Azur • Crete • Cuba • Cyprus • Dominican Republic
Eastern Canada • Eastern USA • Egypt • Florence • Florida • Gran Canaria
Greek Islands/Aegean • Hong Kong • Ibiza/Formentera • Ireland • Israel
Istanbul • Lanzarote • London • Los Angeles • Madeira • Mallorca • Malta • Mexico
Minorca • New York • New Zealand • Normandy • Norway • Paris • Portugal
Prague • Rhodes • Rocky Mountains • Rome • San Francisco • Scotland • South
Africa • Southwestern USA • Tenerife • Thailand • Turkish Coast • Tuscany
USA: New England • USA: Southern States • Venice • Washington D.C.
Western Canada • Western USA

French • German • Italian • Spanish

*Marco Polo would be very interested to hear your
comments and suggestions. Please write to:*

North America:
Marco Polo North America
70 Bloor Street East
Oshawa, Ontario, Canada
(B) 905-436-2525

United Kingdom:
GeoCenter International Ltd
The Viables Centre
Harrow Way
Basingstoke, Hants RG22 4BJ

*Our authors have done their research very carefully, but should any errors or omissions
have occurred, the publisher cannot be held responsible for any injury, damage
or inconvenience suffered due to incorrect information in this guide*

Cover photograph: Costa de Prata, Praia do Areinho (Schlemmer)
Photos: Author (34); Baumli (46); HB-Verlag, Hamburg (22, 28); K. Kallabis (60);
Laif: Osang (12, 24); F. Langer (82); Mauritius: Bordis (50), Dumrath (16), Eichhorn/Zingel (42),
Fagot (70), Hubatka (99), Mayer (84), Rossenbach (4, 20, 79), Susan (30, 76),
Thonig (15), Vidler (26, 36, 55); R. Osang (6, 45, 65)

1st edition 2000
© Mairs Geographischer Verlag, Ostfildern, Germany
Translator: David Cocking
English edition 2000: Margaret Court
Editorial director: Ferdinand Ranft
Chief editor: Marion Zorn
Cartography for the Road Atlas: © Mairs Geographischer Verlag, Ostfildern
Design and layout: Thienhaus/Wippermann
Printed in Germany

Discover Portugal!

The land of the explorers on the western edge of Europe – sunny coasts, Moorish and Christian art

Portugal has been in the EU since 1986, but still little is known in central Europe about this small country and its great history. Portugal is neither an appendage of Spain nor is it just a country somewhere in the ocean. Although the two Atlantic island groups of the Azores and Madeira belong to it they form only just over three per cent of its total area of some 90,000 square kilometres. Portugal lies on the Iberian Peninsula in the extreme south-west of Europe, looks out on the Atlantic and has Spain on its back, so to speak. The 832 kilometre-long Atlantic coast is ideal for holidaymakers: steep cliffs with bizarre rock formations, a foaming sea and long bathing beaches. Portugal has a frontier with Spain some 1300 kilometres long which many Spaniards regard as unnatural. The Portuguese, on the other hand, firmly believe that this boundary was laid out thus by

The Manueline love of decoration leaves its stamp on the cloisters of the Batalha convent

nature and is therefore unshakeable. Anyone coming from bare, grey Castile in spring and crossing the frontier at Guarda, for example, the highest town in Portugal, will be able to substantiate the Portuguese argument: scarcely have you left the foothills of the Serra da Estrela behind you than you enter an evergreen garden favoured with a maritime climate which contrasts sharply with the monotonous Castilian plateau. The borders surrounding Portugal – a rectangle 560 kilometres long and a maximum of 220 kilometres wide – are among the oldest in Europe.

Some ten million people inhabit the country, which is divided by the Serra da Estrela (the Malhao is the country's highest peak at 1991 metres) into two main regions: the north, characterized by its varied scenery, and the monotonous and very flat south. The population is not evenly distributed across the country. More than three million people live in the Lisbon area alone, and Porto (Oporto), the country's second

5

largest city, has more than a million in its immediate catchment area. The industrial region between Setúbal and Santarém has provided work and accommodation to refugees in recent years, producing a disproportionately rapid increase in population. The better working and living conditions in the larger towns and cities, together with emigration, have meant that many districts which were already thinly populated are now almost completely uninhabited: these include the villages and small towns inland along the Spanish border and the settlements in the infertile mountain regions to the north. Today only 35 people per square kilometre still live in these regions. They work mainly in agricultural concerns which, having been handed down through generations, have become so small that they can scarcely provide a living.

In the south, especially in Alentejo, in direct contrast to the small farms in the north, can be found large estates covering more than 3000 hectares. Early in 1975, after the Portuguese Revolution, impoverished land workers occupied these estates and worked them as cooperatives. However, by as early as 1977 most of the seized land had been restored to its owners.

The country enjoys a Mediterranean climate. Annual rainfall, especially in the north, is however appreciably higher than in Mediterranean countries of comparable geographical latitude and even in the summer months there are more than five to seven days of rain. Thus oaks, pines and eucalyptus also grow here. In the

Grape harvest in the land of port wine: the green Douro Valley in northern Portugal

south, on the other hand summers are long and dry and the cork oak predominates. Exotic plants, brought back from voyages of discovery, can today be found both in parks and growing wild and, together with its native flora, have made Portugal the "Garden of Europe".

Even more than for its climate and richly varied vegetation, however, Portugal is known for its history, something the Portuguese are very proud of. They will gladly talk about their traditions: they will refer to the Stone Age finds and the settlements established by the Iberians and Celts between 800 and 500 BC, those former towns of round and oval houses near Braga and Guimarães which are open to visitors.

Both towns were still inhabited when the Romans extended their empire to the Iberian Peninsula. The Romans stayed here for five hundred years, and as well as bringing Roman culture and civilization to Portugal they introduced above all a unified language.

The Germanic tribes, which swarmed over the Pyrenees after the year 410 and did not stop until they reached the Atlantic coast, brought the concept of royal rule to Portugal. The Vandals conquered southern Galicia and founded the kingdom of Portucale with Braga as its capital. Later during the 5th century the Visigoths invaded and brought large parts of Portugal under their yoke.

Three hundred years later the Moors occupied almost the whole of the Iberian Peninsula. In 1713 they took Lisbon and pressed northwards to the Douro.

Towards the end of the 9th century the *reconquista*, the reconquering of the Iberian Peninsula by the Christians, started in the kingdom of León. Knights from the whole of Europe supported this struggle, and the decisive blow was struck under King Alfonso VI (1065–1109): the Moors were forced back behind the Tejo. Following this victory the county of Portucale was divided into Galicia and Portugal, the region between Minho (state border) and Tejo. Count Alfonso Henrique himself pressed his claim for autonomy against his mother, secured independence from the Spanish León-Castile and proclaimed himself the first king of Portugal.

The country prospered under King Dinis (1279–1325) in particular. This upturn lasted until Castile laid claim to the Portuguese throne which led to the battle of Aljubarrota (1383). The monastery at Batalha was built in gratitude for the victory over the Spaniards which secured Portugal's independence.

Under the House of Avia Portugal developed into a world power. An important figure in this was King Henry's son (1394–1460), later nicknamed "The Navigator". Interested in natural science, he founded a school for navigation where the scientific and technical qualifications for voyages of discovery were established. Portuguese conquests in north and west Africa were followed by the discovery of the Azores and Madeira (1432).

About 50 years later Bartolomeo Diaz reached the Cape of Good Hope, and before the end of the century Vasco da Gama sailed round Mozambique and reached India, and Pedro Alvares Cabral discovered Brazil in 1500. No wonder people nicknamed the reigning King Manuel I (1495–1521) "the Fortunate". The "Golden Age" dawned. The arts, sciences, crafts and trade were all nurtured, and Portugal became a world power. However, worldwide colonization and extravagant living at home took their toll. People sought scapegoats for the incipient decline, the Jews were persecuted and the Inquisition was established.

Finally, because the king's grandson had died in Morocco without issue, the upper chamber elected Philip II of Spain as king of Portugal. Under his reign Spanish policy was pursued at Portugal's expense. It was sixty years before a duke drove out the Spaniards and the first regent from the House of Braganza was crowned king in 1640. Absolutist rule in Portugal began. Income from large gold deposits in Brazil helped to put state finances back on a sound footing.

From the mid-18th century the Marquês de Pombal, a benevolent despot, carried out some far-reaching reforms; he promoted schooling, agriculture, commerce and manufacturing and when Lisbon was almost completely destroyed by an earthquake in 1755 he had it rebuilt within a short time. However, the reforms proved short-lived; after the death of José I Portugal joined England and

Spain in the fight against the French.

When the French under Napoleon marched into Portugal in 1807 the royal family fled to Brazil. It was 1811 before the French were driven out with the help of the English, but the liberators remained behind as an occupying force until 1820 when a revolution ended the British occupation. A liberal constitution was drawn up recognizing the king, who had returned from Brazil.

In the 19th century class struggles dominated politics in Portugal. In 1908 King Carlos I was assassinated in Lisbon together with his son, heir to the throne, Luis Filipe. On 5 October 1910 Europe's third republic (after Switzerland and France) was proclaimed. However, it did not bring peace to the country. In 1926 there was a army coup and a military government was set up. António de Oliveira Salazar was appointed Minister of Finance by the new state president António Carmona, and he began to convert Portugal into a Fascist state. In 1932 he became Prime Minister and until 1968 he ruled the country with the aid of the dreaded secret police, the *Pide*, and waged war in the colonies which he colourfully named "overseas provinces". Marcelo Caetano, Salazar's successor, tried to steer a liberal course, but his attempts failed from the outset.

On 25 April 1974 the "Armed Forces Movement" brought down the government. The revolution was broadcast on the radio through the song "Grândola, Vila Morena" by José

History at a glance

200 BC–AD 410
Roman rule

410–711
Germanic invasion – Kingdom of Portugal

from 711
Moors conquer the Iberian Peninsula

750–1250
Reconquista (reconquering by the Christians)

1139–1383
Burgundian (Borgonha) rule – driving out of the Moors, independence from Spain, economic and cultural upswing

1385–1433
King João I and his son Henry the Navigator pursue a policy of expansion – discovery of Madeira and the Azores and of the west coast of Africa – Portugal develops into a world power

1495–1521
King Manuel I – the "Golden Age"; a flowering of art and culture – Cabral discovers Brazil

1580–1640
Spanish rule – oppression and exploitation in the interior – weakening of status abroad, loss of a part of the colonial possessions

17th–19th century
The House of Braganza – wealth from abroad – impoverishment of the people – economic independence from Britain – benevolent despotism under Pombal – French and British occupation – civil war between liberals and absolutists – severance of Brazil

1910
On 5 October a Republic is declared

1910–26
The First Republic – seven parliaments and 45 governments in 16 years – military coup

1928–74
The dictator Salazar – reforming state finances – new constitution – abolition of parliament – appointing a corporative House of Representatives – single party, suppression of democratic rights, resistance in Portugal and in the colonies

1974
25 April military coup – end of dictatorship

Since 1974
A democratic Portugal – socialist efforts – coup attempts – gradual democratization – colonies gain independence

1986
Portugal becomes a member of the EU

1998
Admitted into the European Monetary System – World Exhibition in Lisbon

Afonso a respected member of the opposition to the dictatorship. There was no bloodshed, the populace cheered the soldiers and showered them with red carnations. Caetano and his government offered no resistance. A provisional left-wing government had to withstand sundry attempted coups. However, the moderates retained the upper hand. General Ramalho Eanes remained state president until he was superseded in 1986 by the socialist Marino Soares, who himself was followed by his fellow party member Jorge Sampaio in 1996.

Under various changes of government from 1976 onwards Portugal gradually became a democratic state with a socially conscious market economy. Expo 98 in Lisbon displayed this transformation process to the whole world. The "poorhouse of Europe" had been converted within a quarter of a century to a handsome villa with a view over the Atlantic.

The craft industry, port wine and the cork-oak economy still play their part, but of more importance are questions pertaining to the industrial situation. In order to profit from the low overheads in Portugal international industry is producing all it possibly can, from cars to semiconductors and shoes.

Wine is produced in many areas, but the most important vineyards are in the north with the port wine industry centred on Porto (Oporto).

Tourism is a decisive economic factor – each year some eleven million holidaymakers visit Portugal, giving employment to

600,000 people. The country is making investments: in Alentejo is the largest reservoir in Europe, the rail network is being enlarged, Lisbon's underground railway is being extended, and a new airport and expansion of the motorway network are planned for the future.

Wherever they go tourists can see how much the countryside, climate, history and an open-minded approach to everything new govern the animated approach to life shown by the Portuguese. Although the whole country is equipped with the most modern apparatus, machines and automata the Portuguese still manage to retain their own rhythm. Even though modern tills can add up in seconds the sales girls still take all the time in the world to wrap up their goods slowly and laboriously but lovingly, be it fancy cakes, jewellery or simple fabrics. The harassed central European sees himself transported to another world; his inherent sense of urgency counts for nothing. Time seems to stand still, or at least it cannot be measured in monetary terms.

The visitor is likely to be somewhat disconcerted when he is overtaken in a hair-raising fashion and at high speed on a blind bend and then a little later sees the same car standing near the quayside. The driver and his passenger are sitting calmly gazing through the windscreen at the water, enjoying the play of the waves and listening raptly to the sounds of the sea. Among other things, it adds to the charm of the holiday to observe and admire or smile at this amalgam of the modern and the traditional.

This feeling for life dominates art in Portugal as well as everyday living. At the many festivals, both religious and secular, folk dances are performed accompanied by traditional musical instruments. Only Lisbon and Coimbra are the true home of *fado*, this mysterious and difficult to understand song. Lisbon fado is very different from the Coimbra version. The now worldfamous ensemble "Madredeus" takes folk songs and the *fado* with its impassioned feelings and combines them with elements of rock music in such a way that even the producer Wim Wenders is fascinated by the music and was motivated by it to produce his film "Lisbon Story". Maria Helena Vieira da Silva feels the same, as shown in the way she combines traditions and symbols of ceramic art with modern techniques and strange colours in her work in the Lisbon underground stations.

Literature, too, weaves a new feeling of self-esteem among the Portuguese from living recollections. Whether its Miguel Torga, in his "Tales from the Mountains" or in the "Wine Harvest", describing a world which should not be as it is and at the same time heralding an ethic of solidarity, or Jorge de Sena in "Beacon", contrary to the traditional taboos of Portuguese society, inventing a new language for youthful sexuality, or Lidia Jorge in "Paradise without Borders" encouraging young people who have broken with all convention to seek new ways of self-expression: they all see Portugal as the cradle of a past, present and future world. Even José Saramago, the winner of the 1998 Nobel Prize for Literature, acknowledges in an interview that he is "a product of Portuguese culture, but with very personal convictions" and in his work deals with matters which are "present in one way or another in all Portuguese".

Miguel Torga: "Wine Harvest"

Published back in 1945, this novel conveys to the visitor to Portugal even more of the mentality of the Portuguese than many a wordy travel guide. The novel is set at the time of the wine harvest on the slopes of the Douro. Forty men, women and children have come down from the mountains to work in the blazing hot sun sorting and pressing the grapes in return for meagre wages, wretched food and inferior accommodation. They are employed by the *nouveau riche* upstart Lopes from Oporto, who treats his workers just as inhumanely as his brutal steward Seara. The wife and daughter of the estate owner cannot cope with the sudden riches either. They squander their lives in a state of pious idleness and conceited pride. With "Vindimar" (Wine Harvest) Miguel Torga has written a spiritual story of the Portuguese.

From azulejo to vinho verde

Almost every visitor to Portugal will come across its glazed tiles, its "green" wine and its port wine

Azulejos

The name còmes from the Arabic and broadly means small, polished stone; it refers to the mostly blue and white tiles found in Portugal. They brighten up flat surfaces, reflect light, deaden noise and protect from heat. The Moors brought the painted, glazed tiles into Portugal as long ago as the first century of their campaign of conquest. At that time the ornamentation consisted only of geometric shapes and flower or plant designs, as Islam prohibited the portrayal of figures. It was not until the 16th century that the Portuguese adopted this artistic legacy, and then soon began the era of covering large expanses of walls in churches, monasteries, palaces and country mansions. The pictures portray Christian legends, historical and patriotic events, sea battles, hunting motifs and even small love scenes. After

The ubiquitous Moorish legacy: the mainly blue and white azulejos

the great earthquake of 1755 the minister the Marquês de Pombal arranged for the mass production of practical, long-lasting and hygienic tiles. In the 18th century the production of tiles increased further still: Portugal exported to Brazil, Madeira and the Azores. The art of *azulejos* remains very much alive and popular to this day; just as landscape scenes decorate the walls of houses in Bavaria, for example, so painted tiles gleam on the fronts of numerous new buildings in Portugal.

Luís Vaz de Camões

Hardly any other artist is so firmly embedded in the minds of his compatriots as the author Camões. Lisbon and Coimbra both claim the honour of being his birthplace. In his national epic poem "Os Lusíadas" he powerfully and eloquently praises the voyages of discovery under Vasco da Gama as great Portuguese feats. An indication of the high regard in which he is held is the "Dia de Camões", which is cel-

13

ebrated annually on the 10 June, the day of his death. Camões was born in 1524 or 1525 in Lisbon and received his classical education in Coimbra. Later he went to Lisbon where he got commissions to write plays and poems and was received at court. During war service for the king in Morocco he lost an eye and in 1553 he was made administrator of Portuguese assets in the colonies. In India and Goa he came into conflict with those in power and was banished to the Spice Islands. Recalled to Goa in 1560 his ship found itself in distress. It was with great difficulty that the poet managed to save his life and his recently completed "Os Lusíadas". In 1570 homesickness drove him back to Lisbon where publication of his life's work in 1572 brought him fame but no money. Completely impoverished, he died of the plague in 1579 and was buried in a mass grave.

Europe

For the Portuguese this was always a synonym for a foreign country, somewhere their children went because their homeland could not support them. For centuries Portugal, because of its geographical location, turned its back on Europe and always looked out to sea.

Today the Portuguese remember their old links with France and Britain and look spellbound towards Brussels. Portugal's entry into the EU in 1986 was merely the enactment of steps which had been taken after the revolution. The motives for this latter step were of a political and economic nature. Politically, they

hoped that joining would help secure their democratic and constitutional institutions. Economically, the Portuguese hoped for a long-term improvement and greater stability.

In fact the former poorhouse of Europe has become a prosperous state which has been accepted into the European Monetary Union. At the World Exhibition in 1998 (which was also the 500th anniversary of Vasco da Gama's historic voyage of discovery) Portugal showed that it does look to Europe but that also "the oceans are a legacy for the future". Under this motto, as well as referring to its pioneering role in making discoveries, the country indicated that it had taken on the responsibility of maintaining this legacy.

Fado

The dictator Salazar had every reason to ban what he called the "negroid, uncultured prostitutes' song". It was as if he had foreseen that the fall of his regime would one day be celebrated by a fado singer. Officially he justified the ban on the fado on the morbidly fatalistic behaviour it was supposed to arouse in those listening to it. In actual fact, however, the statesman feared the rousing effect of the songs from Lisbon and Coimbra.

The origin of these folk songs is uncertain. Some say they evolve from the medieval minnelied or Moorish music, others trace them back to coarse sailors' songs or Far Eastern songs of destiny. Catalogues often say that the fado originated in the Old Town of Lisbon. There *fadistas* (female singers) in black dresses sing their melancholy songs by candlelight. Accompanied by two *guitarristas* (melody and rhythm guitars) they appeal to one's sentiments when they sing of unfulfilled longing, of unrequited love and deep despair. The listeners identify themselves with those who are suffering in the song, and the sick condition of the world pains them in the true sense of the word.

It is different in Coimbra, where usually young men sing the fado. Here too it deals with love and death, but misfortune is not attributed to fate or blind destiny but rather to social politics. Feelings of opposition and resistance envelop the listener. It was this kind of fado, which had

become a political song, that Salazar feared, and exactly how justified his fear had become was demonstrated on 25 April 1974 when the song by the fado singer José Afonso "Grândola, Vila Morena" was broadcast by the Catholic radio station as a signal for the outbreak of the revolution which overthrew the hated regime.

Fátima

In 1917 the Virgin Mary appeared to three shepherd children in Cova da Iria, near present-day Fátima. At her sixth and final appearance six months later 70,000 people experienced the "Sun Miracle" when the heavens darkened and rotated like a fiery ball in the firmament. At that

Almost as important as Lourdes: the pilgrimage church in Fátima

time the message of peace of the Virgin Mary was interpreted as a counter-force to the rise in Communism – the revolution had just broken out in Russia. In spite of resistance from the Church, a chapel was built on the site in 1918 and this drew thousands of pilgrims to Fátima every year. Ten years later a start was made on building the basilica and the adjoining great square for prayers which is twice as large as St Peter's Square in Rome. In 1930 the Church officially recognized the veneration of the Virgin Mary. Today Fátima, together with Lourdes and Santiago de Compostela, is one of the most famous places of pilgrimage in Europe.

Supplying the raw material for bottle corks: cork oaks stripped of their bark

Cork oak

Every third bottle cork in the world comes from Portugal and so far there is no better substitute for sealing wine bottles. In the quiet and melancholy countryside in the province of Alentejo grow whole forests of cork oak. In this area, which covers the whole of southern Portugal, stand 86 million specimens of *quercus suber*. The trees attain a height of about 6–10 m and have a life span on average of about 150 years.

Little survives here other than cork oaks and olive trees. When the heat is at its most unbearable is when work begins for those who peel the bark from the cork oaks, for it is then that the metabolism of the trees is at its highest.

The trees must be almost 20 years old before the bark can be peeled off for the first time. With practised blows the men chop two horizontal notches round the trunk and join them with a vertical one. Slowly they loosen the bark with the axe handle until it gives and springs off. The pieces of bark are piled up and then weighed down with stones to flatten them. One peeled and now blood-red trunk will have given some 150 kg of bark, and it will be nine or ten years before it can be stripped again.

In the factory the bark is boiled, pressed, dried and cut into slices. Hollow drills cut plugs from the strips of cork, and these are then smoothed, polished and disinfected. The Portuguese have been exporting bottle corks, which are not exactly cheap, for more than 200 years. They are despatched in sacks of up to 20,000. Germany alone takes 50,000 sacks a year. To safeguard the raw materials long-term new plantations have been planted in recent years with the help of extensive reafforestation aid from Brussels.

Manueline style

Here, too, on the very edge of Europe, can be found the great stylistic trends of European architecture: fortress-like Romanesque churches, great Gothic castles and domes with great stress laid on pointed arches and slender columns, large palaces and mansions of the Renaissance and baroque churches with ormolu woodwork.

Only when the art lover comes to Tomar, or visits Batalha or stands before the Hieronymite convent in Lisbon will he be confused, because the familiar becomes unfamiliar and he is faced with something he has never seen before. Suddenly he will discover the unusual in other places too, here on the doorways and windows, there on columns and staircases: the Manueline style. This unique Portuguese art form developed during the rule of King Manuel I (1495–1521), the Golden Age, when Portugal became a world power. Judged by European standards, the Manueline style is a transition from Late Gothic to Renaissance. It is notable for a delight in decoration, Basic structures and building features from the Late Gothic are ornamented in a way which was not yet to be found elsewhere in European architecture. The sources of this new wealth of forms were many and varied: Moorish, South American, African and Asiatic influences were brought back from the voyages of discovery. Tropical plants, foreign animals, sea creatures (shells, coral, fishes), maritime objects (nautical instruments, masts, anchors, nets, ropes, chains) developed into stone ornamentation and lavishly adorn internal and external walls, doors and windows, staircases and pillars. The component parts of the building almost disappear under the extravagant forms and fantastic riot of ornament: slender Gothic columns become tropical palms, simple windows turn into elaborately chiselled coats of arms and doors become triumphal arches. Although all is taken from the real world and reproduced true to nature in every detail, the adornments bring the decorated surfaces to a different level altogether. They become much more important, they become symbols. Thus the Manueline style is more than just a brief episode in Portugal's cultural history. Like the *fado* and the *saudade* it expresses something of the complex nature of Portuguese thought and feeling: a longing for distance and foreign things, being true in every detail to things close and natural, joy in the thrill of beautiful objects and a serious approach to everyday work.

Port wine

Port wine is an aperitif or desert wine which is 18 to 20 per cent proof. Its area of cultivation lies along the River Douro and begins some 100 kilometres east of Oporto. The roots of the vines burrow down as far as twelve metres into the slaty soil.

Until a few years ago the

grapes, which are harvested when very ripe, were pressed in granite tubs by trampling on them with bare feet. As by this method the pips of the grapes were not squashed the bitter juice they contain did not get into the mash. Nowadays most firms have substituted machinery for this job. After the must has fermented it is transported to the port wine producers in Vila Nova de Gaia. There barrels which are a quarter full of brandy stand ready to be filled.

It was the British who first appreciated the taste of port wine nearly three hundred years ago and it is still as popular today. This is why the wording on the labels are in English. "Vintage Port" grapes come from one particular year and only from the best vineyards. After being stored in barrels "Crusted Port", made from old wines of non-vintage years, is put into bottles where crusts form. "Ruby Port" is a young blended wine with the typical ruby-red colour. "Tawny Port" is a blend of light wines after a long period of storage in barrels and is dry and light in colour. White port is obtained from white grapes after being stored in barrels for two years. Vintners in Vila Nova de Gaia offer guided tours and also sell their wine direct.

Saudade

Saudade is an untranslatable word, as its describes a world of emotions which seems to exist only in Portugal. Fate and feeling, nostalgia, longing and misfortune, all come under what the Portuguese understand by *saudade*. Derived from the Latin *solus*, it is closely linked to the concept of "loneliness and isolation"; from solitariness come thoughts, feelings and longings and also a fatalistic acceptance of what is to be and a sad pleasure in pain and suffering. Thus *saudade* is a permanent condition of dissatisfaction with the world and at the same time finding genuine delight in the many endearing things which surround us.

Language

Portuguese is an original Romance language; it is spoken not only in Portugal but also on the Portuguese Atlantic islands (Azores and Madeira), in Macao (South China), in parts of the former Portuguese colonies (Africa, India, Indonesia) but above all in Brazil. In all some 130 million people speak Portuguese. The language derives from the Lusitanian vulgar Latin; characteristic are the rich tense forms and the many nasal sounds, and some knowledge of Latin or Spanish will be a help in understanding it.

Although some English, Spanish and French is understood, particularly in the tourist areas, it is always appreciated if you try to speak a few words of Portuguese.

Bullfighting

Bullfighting in Portugal, in which the bulls are not killed is far less gory than in Spain, but, is a gloriously colourful spectacle. *Cavalheiros* in court costume enter the arena on fine horses, accompanied by *toureiros*, their assistants. They are followed by the *forcados*, dressed in the costume of cowherds from the Ribatejo – white stockings and shirts, knee-breeches, red jackets. The fight begins with two *toureiros* teasing the bull with their red capes and taking refuge behind a wooden fence when it threatens them. Finally follows the fight between rider and bull: the rider shouts at the bull which charges its opponent, and at the very last moment horse and rider swerve to avoid the collision and the bull simply "gorges" the air. Attack follows attack. The rider also tries to stick decorated darts in the neck of the bull as it passes.

The next part of the fight takes place on foot: eight *forcados* position themselves behind one another and move slowly up to the bull. Their leader wears a green pointed hat and enrages the bull by shouting at it. When the bull charges, the first man leaps high in the air just prior to the collision and lands between its horns. His colleagues throw themselves on the bull and grasp it around the head, neck and body with their bare hands and hold fast until it remains still. The *pega* is ended when, on the word of command, they all let go and run away, and only a *toureiro* is left holding the bull by the tail and allows himself to be dragged around the the the arena by the snorting giant. Cows and oxen finally lead the tired bull from the arena. During the *tourada* eight bulls in all are brought into the ring, each fight lasting twenty minutes.

The season lasts from Easter to October. Admission tickets are divided into three classes: *sol* (sun), *sole sombra* (sun and shade) and *sombra* (shade). You are recommended to get a seat in the shade, because the sun can be very hot and, if it is at an angle, it can get in your eyes and make photography difficult.

Vinho verde

Green wine? Red green wine? The dictionary seems to have gone crazy. Anyone ordering wine in Portugal must first decide whether he wants a fresh, sparkling wine (*verde*) or a mature, full one (*maduro*). The translation of verde is indeed "green", but this actually describes the freshness and youthfulness of the wine and the way in which it is made. The grapes are gathered early and fermented for only a short time, but it goes on fermenting after it has been bottled. While maduro wines are similar in character to Italian, French and Spanish wines, verde wine is very lively, acidic and low in alcohol. It is made from grapes grown mainly in the north, especially in the Minho Valley. On hot days white verde, consumed cold, is delightfully refreshing.

When you have decided whether to ask for *verde* or *maduro*, the waiter will ask whether it is to be red (*tinto*), white (*branco*) or rosé (*rosé*); finally, he will want to know whether the wine should be dry (*seco*) or sweet (*doce*); having then decided whether you wish it served cooled (*fresco*) or at room temperature, the only other thing you must do is decide on the growing region. Excellent *vinhos verde* are pressed from the Alvarinho grape.

Plain cooking in the best tradition

Portuguese cooking is substantial and usually comes in generous helpings

As long as four hundred years ago epicures from central Europe were describing Portuguese cuisine as tasty but not exactly exquisite. In fact it is the precise opposite of *nouvelle cuisine*. There are no tiny portions artistically displayed on a huge plate; Portuguese food is plain and substantial "home cooking" served in generous portions.

As is usual in the countryside, most dishes are based on stews made from leftovers with the addition of herbs such as thyme, bay and rosemary. Fish and pork head the menu; olive oil and garlic govern the taste. The cook may spend hours pot-roasting and simmering – but the result is always a delight.

Eating in Portugal is almost a ritual, when the diners take their time and enjoy conversation. Chatting is as important a part of eating in Portugal as the wine.

A menu begins with small starters (depending on the category of restaurant, the choice

may range from sardines or ham and sharply spiced sausage to lobster) or soup. The commonest soups on a Portuguese menu are *sopa de peixe* (fish soup), *sopa de legumes*, a thick vegetable soup with oil, white wine and mixed spices, and *caldo verde*, a nourishing potato soup with finely cut cabbage and a slice of smoked sausage.

The second course is usually freshly caught or dried fish, eaten boiled, fried or grilled. It always comes with a portion of potatoes and vegetables or salad. Sauces are rarely added.

Shellfish is relatively expensive in Portugal. Portugal's favourite fish (and also a traditional Christmas dish) is *bacalhau*, what we would call dried or salted cod. It does not come from the local coasts but much further north from the waters off Newfoundland.

In the 16th century Portuguese sailors brought it back for the first time; when dried it kept for six months or so. Today it is landed mainly in central Portugal and dried on low racks in the sun. In its raw state it does not look particularly appetising and gives off a strong smell. It

A scene that is now becoming more and more rare: sardines drying in the sun

21

must first be soaked in water for days before it can be prepared. There are said to be at least 365 recipes, one for each day of the year; it is grilled (*grelhado*), boiled (*cozida*), baked (*no forno*) or steamed, broken into pieces or served whole. However, it is always prepared with a generous amount of olive oil; therefore it is not only nutritious but also a heavy dish which needs the accompaniment of rich wine to aid digestion.

As a meat course there is pork, beef, goat, lamb, as well as domestic and wild poultry. A Portuguese speciality is a mixture of fish and meat, e.g. pork with Venus mussels.

Vegetables are not very plentiful – usually potatoes or rice are served with the meat and beans of all varieties are popular.

As regards desserts, it is not easy in Portugal just to be satisfied with cheese or fruit. Sweet dishes and sweet pastries are a Portuguese passion; there are numerous delicacies made with eggs and sugar, almonds, honey, coconut, figs, pumpkins, vanilla and cinnamon, all incredibly sweet. Marzipan is a particular favourite in the Algarve. Recipes and names are equally highly imaginative: heaven's bacon, nun's breast, angels' stomach, marital bed, lovecakes and many more.

Prices

Pricewise Portuguese food, especially in the north of the country, is still somewhat cheaper than in other European countries. There are soups from about $ 308, dish of the day from $ 1,538, fish dishes between $ 1,538 and $ 3,075, a bottle of wine from $ 513, for a coffee you will have to pay between $ 103 and $ 265, while a piece of cake also costs $ 103 to $ 265. In some restaurants you can order half portions (*meia dose*). Many restaurants offer a complete tourist menu (*ementa turística*) including wine and coffee at particularly favourable rates.

Meal times

Lunch: 12.30–3 pm
Evening meal: 7.30–10 pm

Bars and restaurants

The interior of Portuguese restaurants is usually plain and simple; it also keeps very cool because of the tiled decoration, especially in the south of the country, and at first glance somewhat inhospitable. "Cosy" decor with fishing nets and candlelight is found almost exclusively in tourist strongholds. In such (*restaurantes típicos*), however, you will have to pay for the atmosphere. The quality of a restaurant

Nicola, a traditional café on Lisbon's Rossio: hubbub on the terrace, superb art déco inside

should be judged not from its interior fittings but from the number of Portuguese who are eating there.

Apart from the normal *restaurantes* (divided into three classes) there are *churrasqueiras*, restaurants offering fish speciality dishes seafood, *snackbars* with small menus for the guest in a hurry, *tascas*, simple, somewhat shabby pubs with rich and tasty food, *cafés* and *confeitarias* with cakes, sandwiches and light refreshments.

As well as having discovered and learnt to appreciate Portuguese port, the British also share their habit of having a small snack between meals; so the cafés and snack bars offer all kinds of vol-au-vents with fish (*bolinhas de bacalhau*) or meat fillings (*pastéis*), puff pastries with chicken fillings (*empada folhada de galinha*), toasted, buttered white bread (*torrada*) and rolls with steak, ham and mustard (*prego*).

Drinks

As regards wine Portugal is way ahead in the world rankings: this little country in the south-west of Europe is not only one of the biggest wine exporting countries in the world (even though less than ten per cent of the annual production is exported), according to some statistics the annual consumption of wine per head reaches astronomical proportions. Wine is cheap in Portugal. For a glass in a pub you will pay $ 101 to $ 135, for a wine from a good year in a restaurant from $ 1690 a bottle.

In spite of wine being so cheap, beer consumption in Portugal has trebled in the past twenty years. For a long time a glass of beer (*cerveja*) was an object of prestige. A small bottle in a bar now costs from $ 169; if you fancy a small beer it is called a *fino*, a large glass is a *caneca*. The drink on the table is water (*água mineral*) from numerous medicinal springs; price in the restaurant from $ 236 a litre. Tap water can be drunk without any worries. Lemonade and cola are available anywhere; price in a bar or café say $ 169 to $ 270. A coffee with milk (*galão*) is popular during the morning.

The Portuguese will drink a *bica* or *cimbalino*, a small, strong black coffee, at any time of day or night – often standing at a counter or chatting in a café, and frequently accompanied by a "short" of some kind. The Portuguese have an inexhaustible range of the latter; they include *bagaço*, distilled from spent hops, similar to the Italian *grappa*, *ginginha*, a cherry liqueur, *medronho*, a liqueur laced with honey and made from the fruit of the strawberry tree, *amêndoa amarga*, a light, bitter almond liqueur, or *madeira*, an aperitif wine from the terraced slopes of the island of Madeira.

Portugal has a long tradition of bottling mineral water and this can be brought in still or carbonated types. International brands of soft drinks are available as well as local varieties and also freshly pressed fruit juice.

Ceramics, tiles and cork

The traditional craft products are without doubt well worth buying

In Portugal it is becoming more and more difficult to find that relaxed, unspoilt way of life so sought after by tourists. In Lisbon's Baixa, in some small towns, but above all in villages you will come across it from time to time – in the little corner shops and junk shops. Popular souvenirs include basketwork, cane goods, filigree jewellery from Gondomar (near Oporto), ceramic goods, silver and gold jewellery (cheapest in Oporto), corkwork from the Alentejo, costume dolls from Nazaré and, of course, *azulejos*.

Markets and covered markets

Almost every little town in the country has its covered market where you can find fruit, vegetables, flowers, meat and fish. At the weekend markets (in most of the larger towns) there is almost everything from cattle to clothing, vegetables and small furniture to crockery and toilet bowls.

It is wonderful just to rummage around in the little grocery shops, such as those in Lisbon's Baixa

Ceramic goods

There are black (from the mountain regions), red (from the north), white (from the south) and heavily decorated, colourful ceramics (from central Portugal). Factories are scattered across the whole country and some are open to visitors, such as that in Condeixa-a-Nova, about 15 km south of Coimbra.

Embroidery

Portugal is renowned for its handmade tablecloths with artistic lace embroidery. Most come from the Viana do Castelo region, Amarante and from Castelo Branco.

Textiles

In past years textile factories have shot up in the north of Portugal in particular and have made the manufacture of clothing and shoes a major branch of industry. Factory sales are published via the media and tourist information sheets. A wider selection of seconds can be found at the weekly markets.

Pilgrimages and processions

Most Portuguese festivals and celebrations
are religious in origin

PUBLIC HOLIDAYS

1 January (*New Year*)
Carnival Tuesday
Good Friday
25 April (*Anniversary of the Revolution*)
1 May (*Labour Day*)
Corpus Christi
10 June (*National holiday – Dia de Camões*)
15 August (*Assumption*)
5 October (*Republic Day*)
1 November (*All Saints Day*)
1 December (*Independence Day*)
8 December (*Immaculate Conception*)
25 December (*Christmas*)

FESTIVALS & EVENTS

Costa Verde

Holy Week: *Festas da Semana Santa*; processions through the flower-decked streets of Braga

21–23 April: *Romaria do Bom Jesus* in Fão near Esposende; procession and folk festival

Early May: *Festa das Rosas* in Vila

On the second weekend in May a colourful procession in honour of the Madonna of the Roses passes through Vila Franca do Lima near Viana

Franca do Lima; festival in the Minho tradition with folk dancing, bands and fireworks

3–5 June: *Festas do Senhor* in Matosinhos; annual market, folk festival, fair

Corpus Christi processions in Penafiel and Monção

23–24 June: ★ *Festas de São João* in Oporto and Braga. On Midsummer's Eve the town centres are sealed off and there is a great public celebration. The participants hit each other on the head as they pass with garlic sticks and small plastic hammers. It ends with a grand fireworks display.

17–20 August: ★ *Romaria de Nossa Senhora da Agonia* in Viana do Castelo; the region's largest popular festival is held in and near the Baroque church.

Montanhas

30 April: *Romaria da Senhora do Almurtão* in Idanha-a-Nova; procession and popular celebration

3 May: *Festival of the Cross* or *Festival of the Senhora do Castelo* in Monsanto. It celebrates victory at the end of a long siege. The enemy were outwitted by

27

a fatted calf thrown down from the town walls. To the beat of drums and old songs women climb the castle walls and throw down flower pots and a replica of a calf.

5 July–5 August: *Feira de São Tiago* in Mirandela

25–26 August: *Festas de Santa Bárbara* in Miranda do Douro

Early September: *Pilgrimage* to the church of *Senhora dos Remédios* in Lamego. Every year thousands of believers come to this church which is dedicated to the Virgin Mary. At the beginning of September the stream of pilgrims grows, there are large processions and the pilgrimages become a popular celebration.

Costa de Prata

February: *Festa de São Grao* in Nazaré; on the Saturday before Shrovetide there are processions in the little wood near Nazaré. Many people come in disguise; it all ends with a grand picnic in the wood.

Holy Week: *Festas da Semana Santa* in Óbidos; procession

12–13 May: *Pilgrimage* in Fátima

At Whitsun the four-day *Festival of the Tabuleiros* is celebrated in Tomar, the town of the Order of the Knights Templar.

At many festivals you can witness bull fights, which in Portugal do not end with the bull being killed

Loaves of bread decorated with flowers and ribbons are blessed in front of the parish church and then carried in procession through the streets by young girls dressed in white. This is followed by folklore events, a craft market and fireworks.

Middle of June: *Festival of the Holy Ghost* in front of the convent in Batalha. This festival has a 400 year-old tradition. In the "donation procession" maidens carry the

---

MARCO POLO SELECTION: FESTIVALS

1 Viana do Castelo
Romaria de Nossa Senhora da Agonia (third week in August) with folklore, costumes and fireworks (page 27)

2 Oporto (Porto)
Festas de São João, a unique and grand popular festival on Midsummer's Eve (page 27)

> ### In the spirit of Marco Polo
>
> Marco Polo was the first true world traveller. He travelled with peaceful intentions forging links between the East and the West. His aim was to discover the world and explore different cultures and environments without changing or disrupting them. He is an excellent role model for the travellers of today and the future. Wherever we travel we should show respect for other peoples and the natural world.

sanctified gifts to the church on their heads. The celebrations are accompanied by folklore productions.

12–13 October: *Pilgrimage* in Fátima

Lisbon and its surroundings

June: Month of *street festivals* in Lisbon; ask for *arraiais* (festival grounds)

13 June: *Festas dos Santos Populares* in Lisbon

29 June: *Festa de São Pedro* in Sintra

30 June–2 July: *Festas do Colete Encarnado* in Vila Franca de Xira (with bull fights)

5 July–28 August: *Feira do Artesanato de Estoril*; folk art market/fair

On the first weekend in August the *Festival of Nossa Senhora da Boa Viagem* is held in Peniche. When night falls decorated boats sail out to sea in honour of the patron saint of the fishermen of Peniche.

8–11 September: *Festas da Senhora da Boa Viagem* in Moita (with bull fights)

Planícies

On Easter Monday in Constância, where the rivers Tejo and Zêzere meet, dozens of bedecked ships assemble and participate in the procession in honour of *Nossa senhora da Boa Viagem*.

1–10 June: *Feira Nacional da Agricultura* in Santarém; agricultural fair

24–29 June: *Feira de São João* in Évora

10–15 August: *Feira de Agosto* in Beja

Algarve

January: *Almond Blossom Festival* in Vilamoura

Shrovetide: *Festas do Carnaval* in Loulé

Easter: *Romaria da Senhora da Piedade* in Loulé; procession

On Easter Sunday the *Festival of the Floral Torches* is held in São Brás de Alportel. Men run through the streets carrying torches decorated with flowers shouting "Hallelujah". In front of the church they scatter the flowers in the street so that the priest can walk over them with the Blessed Sacrament.

On 14 and 15 August the *Festival of the Senhora da Orada* is celebrated in Albufeira. Fishermen carry the statues of their patron saint to the beach so that she can bless the sea. This is accompanied by markets and dancing events.

The Green Coast: Portugal's most beautiful scenery

The north of the country offers beautiful beaches and an interesting hinterland

This region fully deserves its name – the Green Coast. The Atlantic climate and only two or three months (June–August) without rain and the rivers Minho, Lima, Cavado, Tâmega and Douro all help to produce a noticeably green landscape which is praised by many visitors as being the most beautiful in Portugal.

The peasant farmers, very few of whom can call their land their own, utilize every square metre to grow maize, wheat, potatoes and the tall, long-stemmed species of cabbage which form a basic ingredient of the soup *caldo verde*. The vines, the grapes of which produce the delectable *vinho verde*, grow so tall up trees, poles and granite posts that ladders are needed to prune them and to harvest the grapes. In spite of the proximity of the sea few people gain their living from fishing which today, in contrast to the old days, is done from motor-powered boats with modern equipment. In spite of the hard work involved the

This baroque Stations of the Cross staircase leads up to the church of Bom Jesus do Monte at Braga

---

Hotel and restaurant prices

Hotels
Category 1: over $ 16,400 (Escudos)
Category 2: $ 9,225 to $ 18,450
Category 3: up to $ 10,250
The prices are per night incl. breakfast for two people sharing a double room.

Restaurants
Category 1: over $ 6,150
Category 2: $ 3,075 to $ 6,150
Category 3: up to $ 3,075
The prices are for a meal with starter, main course and dessert without drinks.

MARCO POLO SELECTION: THE COSTA VERDE

1 Sandy beach in Ofir
Extensive beach with dunes
and pine forest (page 35)

2 Barcelos market
Famous for its ceramics
and carved yokes for
oxen (page 34)

3 Bom Jesus do Monte
Pilgrimage church near
Braga with a monumental
"Stations of the Cross"
staircase (page 34)

4 Peneda-Gerês
National Park
Experience nature in its
original form and wild
beauty (pages 35 and 41)

5 Sport and fun in Espinho
Long, sandy beaches
ideal for bathing, together
with golf courses, gambling
casinos and night-clubs for
entertainment
(page 39)

inhabitants, most of whom live in small houses made of granite, still abide by old customs; it is a very special experience to join in the popular festivals with their lively folk dancing. However, this does not disguise the fact that poverty has forced thousands to emigrate. Nevertheless, strong industrial development and a growth in tourism have produced an economic upswing in this region as well.

BRAGA

(100/C4) Anyone approaching Braga, Portugal's fourth largest town, from the sea will pass through evergreen hilly countryside; smallholders cultivate the fields which are separated one from the other by granite walls. For them and for the 170,000 inhabitants of the town Braga is the very centre of the universe. This is not just because "Bracara Augusta" was the major traffic centre in northern Portugal back in the times of the Romans and the Moors, and not because kings resided here at times during the Middle Ages. Braga can attribute its standing to the high-ranking dignitaries, the archbishops, who determined the fortunes of the region as advisers and intermediaries of those holding positions of power, but who often also opposed the latter and acted in an independent manner. The large number of clergy were also always opposed by secular elements, and so it comes as no surprise to find department stores and factories side by side with the 20 churches and palaces from the Middle Ages and the Baroque period.

SIGHTS

Antigo Paço Episcopal
Bibliophiles will be overwhelmed by the plethora of books, especially old manuscripts, in the large library in the former episcopal palace. *Open Mon–Fri 9 am–6 pm, admission free, Rua do Souto*

Palácio dos Biscainhos

Walking through the town visitors will be struck again and again by the large, granite-built manor houses *(solares)* and town houses. Worth seeing are the *Casa de Avelar* (external viewing only) and the Palácio dos Biscainhos *(museum)*. Open Tue–Sun 10 am–midday and 2–5 pm, admission $ 400, Rua dos Biscainhos

Sé (Cathedral)

In the centre of the Old Town the cathedral towers over the surrounding houses. Only the main door arch and the beautiful *south door* still survive from the 11th and 12th century Romanesque church. Otherwise constant changes and renovations have produced a church in which all architectural styles can be studied.

The octagonal Manueline *font* inside, the *organ* richly decorated with allegorical figures and the stone *high altar* with depictions of the Ascension of Christ, together with the two *figures of the Virgin Mary* (Santa Maria de Braga inside and the nursing Mother of God outside on the rear wall of the choir) are the pride and joy of every inhabitant of Braga.

Also beautiful are the the the two cloisters: the *Capela da Glória*, decorated with coats-of-arms and tile-pictures, and the Gothic *Capela dos Reis*.

MUSEUM

Museu de Arte Sacra

A treasure chamber, a Museum of Sacred Art and burial chambers adjoin the cathedral. Here, in addition to the church treasures, can be found all the objects used in Christian liturgy: chasubles, vessels of all kinds, chalices, crucifixes and pictures. However, the presentation is somewhat dismal. Our tip: the Baroque choir stalls and two organs (18th century) which are played every Sunday in the 11 am service. Also worth viewing are the three burial chambers, especially the Baroque tomb of the first bishop of Braga, St Geraldo, which resembles a gilded high altar and contrasts with the walls of the chamber which are clad with sober *azulejos*. Open Tue–Sun 9 am–midday and 2–5 pm, admission $ 300, near the cathedral

RESTAURANTS/CAFÉS

Braga cuisine is governed by the proximity of the sea and the fertile fields around the town. Fish and fruits of the sea are on every menu. Specialities of this region are baked dried cod, meat and vegetable stew *(cozido à portuguesa)* and roast kid *(cabrito assado)*. Cabbage soup *(caldo verde)* with smoked sausage and maize bread *(broa)* was indeed at one time the food of the poorer classes, but it can nevertheless be recommended as being a typical pan-cooked dish. In Braga people have a predilection, not to say a passion, for sweet things: you should definitely try *toucinho do céu* (heavenly bacon), *rabanadas* (poor knights) or *bolo do rei* (regal cakes).

Café Lusitana

✪ For centuries this has been the best café, always full to overflowing but with the best snacks. *Rua Justino Cruz/Jardin de Santa Bárbara*

An autumn snack: roast chestnuts on Barcelos market

A Ceia

Good value, with cuisine typical of the region. *Rua do Raio, Tel. 253/239 32, Category 2*

O Inácio

Popular inn and relatively good value. *Campo das Hortas 4, Tel. 253/61 32 35, Category 2*

ACCOMMODATION

Castelo do Bom Jesus

Individualists will enjoy this picturesque little castle on the hill of the same name; it has 13 lovingly furnished rooms and a swimming pool. *Monte do Bom Jesus, Tel. 253/67 65 66, Fax 67 76 91, Category 1–2*

Hotel do Parque

An exclusive establishment standing high up on Monte do Bom Jesus. Meals are taken in the Hotel do Elevador opposite. From the ☝ dining room there is a magnificent view over Braga. *50 rooms, Monte do Bom Jesus, Tel. 253/67 65 48, Fax 67 66 79, Category 1*

Residencial São Marcos

Clean, somewhat simple, but can be thoroughly recommended. *13 rooms, Rua de São Marcos 80, Tel. and Fax 253/27 71 77, Category 3*

INFORMATION

Turismo

Av. da Liberdade 1, Tel. 253/26 25 50, Fax 61 33 87

SURROUNDING AREA

Barcelos (100/B 4)

Anyone going to the ★ Barcelos market on Thursdays should make a small detour of 4 km and visit the pre-Romanesque/ Byzantine church of *São Frutuoso* (7th century). Worth visiting in Barcelos are the typically Portuguese Baroque church of *Bom Jesus da Cruz*, the *Regional Museum*, the *Ducal Palace* and the old *Jewish Quarter*. At the market you can buy very cheaply the famous cockerel souvenirs, pottery, carvings and basketry as well as leather goods and textiles. In the *Restaurante Dom António (Rua Dom António Barroso, Tel. 253/81 22 85, Category 2)* the cuisine is good; the *bacalhau à Dom António, arroz de marisco* can be recommended.

Bom Jesus do Monte (100/C 4)

★ ☝ 7 km from Braga lies the pilgrimage church of Bom Jesus do Monte with baroque steps, designed as cloisters, leading up to it. From the top there is a magnificent view. After leaving the church 10 km south-east via *Sameira*, a pilgrimage site in monumental style, to *Citânia de Briteiros*, a small Celto-Iberian settlement (c. 800 BC).

Esposende and Ofir   (100/B 4)

From Braga it is not far to Esposende on the coast, where the Cávado flows into the ocean. The fine ★ sandy beach stretches from Ofir at its southern end via Apúlia to Póvoa de Varzim and Vila do Conde, where it is broken up here and there by cliffs and rocks. Close to the beach, between pinewoods and the sea, lies the large *Hotel Sopete Ofir (191 rooms, Av. Raul Sousa Martins, Tel. 253/98 98 00, fax 98 18 71, Category 2)* with a restful ambience and parklike gardens. Between Apúlia and Ofir several ethnic fish restaurants lie close to the sea. For its excellent sardines you are recommended to try the *A Cabana (Lugar Cedovem, Tel. 253/98 20 65, Category 3)*.

Guimarães   (100/C 5)

Visitors should spend at least a day here in the "Cradle of the Nation" (Afonso Henriques, the first king of Portugal, was born here in 1111). A visit to the *castle* (bronze figure of the king by Soares dos Reis), and the *palace* of the Dukes of Bragança is a must. Also recommended are the *Museu de Alberto Sampaio*, primarily because of the gold and silver work, and the *Museu Martins Sarmento*, which houses many finds from the Citânia de Briteiros. *Castle and palace open daily 9 am–5 pm, admission $ 400; Museu de Alberto Sampaio open Tue-Sun 10 am–12.30 pm and 2–5.30 pm, until 7 pm July and* *Aug, admission $ 250, Sun admission free; Museu Martins Sarmento Tue–Sun 9.30 am–midday and 2–5 pm, admission $ 300; restaurant: El Rei, Praça São Tiago 20, Tel. 253/41 90 96, Category 2; hotel; Hotel Toural, 31 rooms, Largo do Toural, close up against the old town wall, newly furnished, Tel. 253/51 71 84, Fax 51 71 49, Category 2*

Peneda-Gerês National Park   (101/D 3–4)

★ A drive along the N 103 from Braga into the Peneda-Gerês National Park is a delight. Before driving up to the *Barragens* (artificial lakes) you should enjoy the view of the stunning landscape from the 🔊 terrace of the Pousada de São Bento (by the N 304 near Caniçada).

PORTO (OPORTO)

(100/B 6) Oporto, together with Rotterdam, is to be a European City of Culture in 2001 and has also been declared a Cultural Heritage site by UNESCO. It has an enchanting setting on the Douro river and those wishing to see its most beautiful side should drive along the upper lane of the Ponte de Dom Luís I to the former convent of Nossa Senhora da Serra do Pilar in Vila Nova de Gaia. From here there is a magnificent view of the country's second largest city (Pop. c.350,000) sitting proudly on a granite cliff high above the steep river bank. Five bridges span the Douro, and below are the old railway bridge built by Gustave Eiffel and the Ponte de Dom Luís I with its two traffic lanes lying one above the other. On the far bank, houses with colourful washing hung out to dry come down almost to the water's edge, being separated from it only by a road. The houses behind cling like swallows' nests to the cliff at the top of which towers Oporto's proud cathedral.

SIGHTS

Azulejos
In Oporto there are many *azulejo*-covered buildings, for example, the *Estação de São Bento railway station concourse*, the external façade of the *Capela das Almas*, the *Igreja do Carmo* and the cloisters of the *Sé* (cathedral). Modern tile-pictures can be found in the *Túnel da Ribeira* (on the bank of the Douro). An informative brochure with details of an *azulejo tour* can be obtained free of charge from the *Turismo* office.

Casa do Vinho Verde
In this 18th century palace visitors can experience all aspects of this sparkling wine. *Open daily 11 am–8 pm, admission free, Rua da Restauração 318*

Cedofeita
Oporto's oldest church. No side-aisles, no decoration, built of grey granite, it still communicates something of the pious spirit of a long-lost age. *Rua Alvares Cabral.*

Foz do Douro
Here, close to the sea, was where the rich people of the city once resided. A stroll along the esplanade of the *Castelo do Queijo* to the mouth of the Douro is well worthwhile. Do not forget to have a drink in one of the cafés close to the pier (*Praia do Molhe).*

Igreja da Misericórdia
Do not fail to visit the Misericórdia church to see its famous 16th century picture of the "Fons Vitae". *Rua das Flores*

Igreja de São Francisco
A stone's throw from the Stock Exchange. The 14th century Gothic style is recognisable only from outside; on entering the church, however, the visitor is overwhelmed by the lavish splendour of the *talha dourada* (the typical Portuguese baroque style, with wood carvings embel-

A view of Oporto from the banks of the port wine river, the Douro

lished with gold leaf) on the two carved altars; pride of possession of Brazilian gold has here developed into a decorative art.

Ribeira Quarter

Narrow lanes, grimy corners, begging children and pathetic little shops: poverty and wealth, glamour and despair rub shoulders in this the most confined district in Oporto. On the *Praça Infante Dom Henrique* stands the *Stock Exchange*, one of the sights in the rich commercial city of Oporto. The ⚹ *Praça da Ribeira* close by the river is the "in" place for young people to meet after 11 pm at weekends.

Tours

The *Turismo* office can supply free of charge detailed suggestions for tours of the city. They concentrate on the medieval, baroque or neo-classical, according to your choice.

Sé (Cathedral)

The Cathedral has almost completely lost its original character as a 12th century fortified church. Renovations, especially in the 18th century, have created a somehow less inspiring picture. Therefore the best thing to do is to view straight away the famous *silver altar* in the sacramental chapel in the north aisle, on which the most famous silversmiths and goldsmiths in Oporto worked for 100 years. Also worth seeing is the Gothic *cloister* with tile-pictures portraying the Song of Songs and Ovid's Metamorphoses, and the extraordinary organ in the front left of the choir.

Torre dos Clérigos

◁▷ The tallest church tower in Portugal is also a symbol of Oporto. View over the city, river and sea near the superbly laid out *Praça da Liberdade.*

MUSEUMS

Fundação de Serralves

A must: museum of modern art in a magnificent park. *Open Tue–Sun 10 am–7 pm, admission $ 800, Rua D. João de Castro 210*

Museu do Carro Eléctrico

The history of trams in Oporto; old trams which have been lovingly restored. Well worth a visit. *Open Tue–Sun 9.30 am–1 pm and 3–8 pm, admission $ 350, Rua Bazílio Teles 51, right on the banks of the Douro*

Museu Nacional de Soares dos Reis

Pre- and early historical finds, Portuguese paintings and sculptures in Portugal's oldest public museum. Our suggestions: the sculptures by Soares dos Reis (1847–89), above all: Desterrado (marble), Pescador, Música, Riqueza and Narciso (all in bronze). *Open Tue 2–6 pm, Wed.–Sun 10 am–6 pm, admission $ 350, Rua Dom Manuel II*

RESTAURANTS & CAFÉS

The people of Oporto are known as *tripeiros* (eaters of entrails), a nickname they acquired in the 14th century when they provided all their stocks of fish for an expedition by Henry the Navigator and kept only the offal for themselves.

Today no visitor to Oporto must leave without trying *tripas à moda do Porto* (giblets, chicken meat, sausage, bacon, white beans, spices). The most popular restaurant district lies in the Ribeira Quarter right by the Douro *(Cais da Ribeira)*. The food here is good (speciality: fresh fish) at, for example, the *D. Tônho* or in the *Mercearia*.

Churrascaria Central dos Clérigos
A typical corner inn with an *azulejo*-decorated dining room. *Rua da Fábrica 69, Tel. 22/200 80 77, Category 3*

Don Manoel
◁▷ High-class, in a stylish villa in Foz do Douro with sea views. *Av. Montevideu 384, Tel. 22/617 23 04, Category I*

O Escondidinho
First-class cuisine, rustic atmosphere. Book in advance! *Rua de Passos Manuel 144, Tel. 22/200 10 79, Category 1*

Majestic Café
The most beautiful coffee house anywhere in the city. *Rua de Santa Catarina 112*

Portofino
In Foz do Douro, discreetly refined but still typical nonetheless. *Rua do Padrao 103, tel. 22/617 73 39, Category 2*

Ideal for a stroll: *Rua de Santa Catarina* with lots of shops, boutiques, cafés and the new *Via Catarina* shopping centre. Indoor markets: *Mercado do Bolhao (city*

centre) and *Mercado do Bom Sucesso (Rotunda da Boavista)*. Shoes and leather goods can be found mainly in the *Rua de Cedofeita* and *Rua Santo António*. Gold and silversmiths' shops are concentrated in *Rua das Flores*. North Portugal's largest shopping centre is *Gaia Shopping* with 170 shops *(Vila Nova da Gaia, on the A 1)*.

Hotel da Boa-Vista
Tasteful hotel in Foz do Douro with charm and a view of the mouth of the Douro. *39 rooms, Esplanada do Castelo 58, Tel. 22/618 00 83, Fax 617 38 18, Category 2*

Hotel Infante de Sagres
The city's best hotel, stylish and elegant. *72 rooms, Praça D. Filipa de Lencastre 62, Tel. 22/200 81 01, Fax 205 49 37, Category 1*

Pensão Rex
Simple, but in a beautiful old residence. *21 rooms, Praça da República 117, Tel. 22/200 45 48, Fax 208 38 82, Category 3*

O Mal Cozinhado (Rua do Outerinho 11) offers the best fado in the city. Minimum charge $ 5,000. There are bars and discotheques at *Rua Passeio Alegre 553 and 1000; Trintaeum 31* (tasteful bar, mostly older clientele), *River* (high-tech bar), *Macedo* (smart restaurant and bar) and *Twin's* (on three floors). New Wave in the *Quando Quando* night spot *(Av. do Brasil 60)*. "In" place for young people: ✠ *Praça da Ribeira*; many cafés, bars, pubs – but nothing gets going before 11 pm!

Turismo
Praça D. João I 43, Tel. 22/205 75 14, Fax 205 32 12

SURROUNDING AREA

Douro Valley (100/B-C 6, 101/D-E 6)
Before going to *Vila Nova de Gaia* to visit a port wine lodge it is recommended that you travel into the Douro Valley to get to know the region where the wine comes from. You can go by rail or by ship to *Peso da Régua*. Another possibility is to take the train near the mouth of the Rio Tua into the Douro and there change to the narrow gauge railway to Mirandela, and come back by bus. If time is short you should at least take a short cruise on the Douro. Departure: Cais da Ribeira or Cais da Estiva.

Espinho (104/B 1)
If you are tired of the city and would like to relax for a few hours why not drive south to the long sandy beaches of Miramar (small church on a rock which is buffeted by the sea), Granja and Espinho. Those going to the ever more modern-looking ★ *Espinho* with its large hotels, night clubs and casinos should first stop at the railway station in *Granja* and see the splendid *azulejos* with pictures of various Portuguese towns. On Espinho's beautiful beach you will find Europe's second largest golf course, the *Oporto Golf Club*.

Matosinhos (100/B 6)
This port and industrial town (fish canning, refineries) is worth

a visit to see the beautiful baroque church of *Bom Jesus*. In the evenings you can dance the night away in the *Buffalos* and *Cais 477* discotheques.

VIANA DO CASTELO

(100/B 3) Monte Santa Luzia towers over the town. Visitors go to the top (by car or mountain railway) not so much to see the neo-Byzantine pilgrimage church but rather because of the Celto-Iberian Citânia and, above all, for the view over the town (Pop. c.16,500), which was named the "Beautiful Town" even before Roman times: visitors can look down on the 736 m long, double-decked iron bridge which Gustave Eiffel built over the Lima, on the harbour on which the wealth of the town was founded, on the new marina and on the roofs of the granite buildings and the proud and beautiful *solares.* manor houses from the "Golden Age".

SIGHTS

Castelo de São Tiago da Barra
During your visit you should walk round the walls of the old fortress. *South-west of the town centre*

Igreja Nossa Senhora da Agonia
Anyone who is in Viana between 17 and 20 August should make a point of visiting the baroque church; this is when the famous Romaria, popular because of its folk festival nature, is held. *Rua de Monserrate*

Igreja São Domingos
On the way to the regional

museum in the western part of town it is worth taking a look in this church to see the over-ornate baroque altar with its typical *talha dourada* (gilded woodcarving).

Praça da República (market place)

Because of its self-contained location this square is one of the most attractive in Portugal. In the centre stands the beautiful, triple *basin fountain*, built by João Lopes-o-Velho in 1551. Although only the façade with doorway and three truncated arches remains of the Gothic *town hall*, this granite edifice decorated with the Manueline coat-of-arms (globe and caravel) has become the symbol of Viana do Castelo. To the left stands the *Casa da Misericórdia* (formerly the hospice), a 16th century Renaissance building. Most impressive are the caryatids, female figures, which support the second and third floors of the palace. The *Misericórdia Church*, built in 1559 by João Lopes-o-Moço, is famous for its vivid *azulejos* in the interior. When the church door is locked the key can be obtained in the ground floor of the Casa da Misericórdia.

A few steps further on is the church of *Matriz (Rua de Sacadura Cabral)*, built in the Gothic period (1400–40), but with the solid, castellated towers and the broad rosette over the doorway clearly reflecting the spirit of the Romanesque. The Manueline archway in the interior and the large model of a ship in the *Capela dos Navegantes* (left transept) make a visit inside a worthwhile experience. Near the church stands the *Casa de João Velho*, the residence of a 15th century merchant, and also known as the *Casa dos Arcos* because of its arcaded arches. The *Rua da Bandeira* with its many boutiques and cafés is inviting.

Museu Municipal

This regional museum is renowned above all for its *azulejos* which were painted by Policarpo de Oliveira in the 18th century and which can be found in the largest room. The pictures portray Europe, America, Africa and Asia in allegorical form. In addition, however, the museum contains ceramics, sculptures, paintings, weapons and choice items of furniture from all over the world. *Open Tue–Sun 9 am–midday and 2–4 pm, admission $ 200, Largo São Domingo*

Costa Verde

✦ A restaurant which is highly regarded by the locals. *Rua de Monserrate 411–413, Tel. 258/82 92 40, Category 2*

Cozinha das Malheiras

Best restaurant in town. *Rua Gago Coutinho 19, Tel. 258/82 36 80, Category 2*

3 Potes

✦ Rustic. Fado music every Friday. *Beco dos Fornos 7–9, Tel. 258/82 99 28, Category 2*

Pensão-Restaurante Guerreiro

Simple rooms, good food, very good value. *17 rooms, Rua Grande 14, Tel. 258/82 20 99, Category 3*

Pousada do Monte Santa Luzia

꙳ Standing on the hill of the same name, this hotel offers not only solid hospitality but also commands a magnificent view of countryside, town and ocean. *55 rooms, Tel. 258/82 88 89, Fax 82 88 92, Category 1*

Hotel Viana Sol

Modern and tastefully furnished (sauna, squash courts, swimming pool, fitness room). *65 rooms, Largo Vasco da Gama, Tel. 258/82 89 95, Fax 82 89 97, Category 2*

ENTERTAINMENT

At first glance there does not seem to be much going on in Viana in the evenings. However, in the discotheques in the large hotels, especially in the *Viana Sol*, it is all happening. Younger people meet in the ꙳ *Nasoni*, in the ꙳ *Indian Bar* and in the ꙳ *Glamour*. We recommend the typical folklore festivals which are held from time to time on private quintas, for example, on the *Quinta do Santoinho, Darque, Tel. 258/240 81.*

INFORMATION

Turismo

Rua do Hospital Velho, Tel. 258/82 26 20, Fax 82 78 73

SURROUNDING AREA

Peneda-Gerês   (100/C 2–3,
National Park   101/D 2–3)
★ A journey east takes you through beautiful countryside by way of *Ponte de Lima* (**100/B 3**) with its interesting bridge, rustic but fine manor houses and *Ponte da Barca* (**100/C 3**) with its little Romanesque chapel and pretty promenade by the river, into the national park with the rivers Lima, Homem and Cávado which are dammed to form large lakes for producing electric power. This wild, hilly countryside with its waterfalls, lush vegetation and rich fauna will inspire the nature lover.

Caminho, Monte Santa Tecla and
Valença do Minho   (100/B 2)
A trip north from Viana do Castelo along the coast as far as Valença do Minho (50 km), where the border with Spain is marked, is a rather special experience. The striking green landscape, intensively worked, contrasts with the grey, granite villages and the foaming white of the sea. Near *Âncora* the visitor can admire the *large stone tomb* of Barrosa dating from the Late Stone Age and the *Caminha* in *Matriz*, probably the most beautiful 16th century church in Minho. From here visitors can cross over into Spanish Galicia on the passenger ferry and visit the ꙳ Celtic settlement with over 1000 round houses on *Monte Santa Tecla*; magnificent view of the mouth of the Minho.

Visitors to Valença do Minho will be richly rewarded by the view from the impressive ꙳ fortifications down onto the bridge and beyond to the Spanish Tui and the countryside on the far side of the river which marks the frontier. A stroll through the romantic old streets is worthwhile not only because of the many small restaurants but also the shops which sell cotton goods at bargain prices.

Beyond the mountains, in port wine country

The peasant farmers in Trás-os-Montes and Beira Alta manage to wrest a variety of crops from the barren soil

The bleak mountain countryside north of Douro, where vines for port wine are cultivated, is not climatically influenced by the sea as much as the rest of Portugal, but has a rather continental climate; long, hot summers and short, cold winters. To the south of the "gold river" (*ouro*, Portuguese for gold) as far as the Serra da Estrela, too, the landscape remains barren and stony. Nevertheless, everywhere that rocky massifs do not prevent it, vineyards and gardens are laid out and olive trees seem to grow even on stones.

There, where the Vouga, the Mondego and the Dão (known for the heavy Dão wines) flow westwards, begin the extensive forests of oaks, chestnuts and pines. Here, in the region with the most water anywhere in Portugal, a dispute has flared up over the eucalyptus tree, "Portugal's green crude oil". Paper manufacturers, who have great influence in this part of the country, have cut down whole forests of oak trees and planted quick-growing eucalyptus trees, Environmentalists are concerned about the effect on the soil, water table and wildlife.

The progress Portugal has made in the economic sphere following its entry into the European Union is demonstrated by the many new buildings and the motorway which runs through the mountains from Aveiro as far as the Spanish frontier near Vilar Formoso. Since 1994 the "Programme for the Revival of Historic Villages" has also received EU support. It has declared the prettiest villages in the countryside surrounding the Serra da Estrela to be cultural assets and wants to make them fit for the youth of the country, who are moving away, to live in.

The medieval castle of Bragança with its massive Torre de Montagem towers protectively over the town

BRAGANÇA

(102/C 3) The road from Chavers along the Parque Natural de Montezinho is very winding. It takes three hours to cover a distance of barely 100 km. Nature lovers, however, will find rewarding the stretch through the national park to Bragança (Pop. c.20,000), the ancestral seat of the royal house of the same name.

SIGHTS

Old Town
The town is dominated by the medieval castle with its impregnable walls around the massive ◁▷ *Torre de Menagem*. Of interest are the tall pillory (*pelourinho*) and the *Domus Municipalis*, an example of Roman civil architecture. In the centre of the town stands the *cathedral* with a brick-built cloister.

RESTAURANT

Restaurante Marisqueira
Simple, cheap establishment. In spite of its maritime name, its speciality is rissoles. *Av. do Sabor, Tel. 273/224 94, Category 3*

ACCOMMODATION

Hotel Braganço
A comfortable, middle-class hotel with attentive service. *42 rooms, Av. Dr. Francisco Sá Carneiro, Tel. 273/33 15 78, Fax 33 12 42, Category 2*

INFORMATION

Turismo
Av. do 25 Abril, Tel. 273/33 10 78, Fax 33 19 13

SURROUNDING AREA

Chaves (101/F 3)
This little spa town appears from a distance to be somewhat plain and dull and swallowed up by the modern high-rise buildings, but nevertheless a stroll through the Old Town, the castle park and along the hot springs is not to be missed. It is also worthwhile climbing up to the massive ◁▷ *14th century castle*, with a magnificent view of the town and surroundings. In the castle: *military museum (open Tue–Sun 2–5.30 pm, admission $ 100)*. On the *Largo das Caldas* there are many restaurants; the *Carvalho (Tel. 276/32*

17 27, Category 2–3) is recognized as the best restaurant in northern Portugal. Superb service is provided in the hotel *Forte de São Francisco, (58 rooms, Forte de São Francisco, Tel. 276/33 37 00, Fax 33 37 01, Category 1)*, which combines modern comforts in harmony with the past. The 17th century castle has been carefully and tastefully restored and provides a stylish ambience for the guests.

Vila Real   (101/E 5)

Like many towns in northern Portugal Vila Real (Pop. 14,000), with its overdeveloped suburbs and impersonal high-rise buildings, appears rather uninviting. However, the centre of the town has retained its old charm. Some 16th and 18th century burghers' houses bear witness to grander times. Vila Real has become known for its black earthenware. If you wish to see where Mateus Rosé comes from you should visit the baroque mansion on the *wine-producing estate of the Mateus family* 4 km to the east. There is a beautiful drive from Vila Real

through the wildly romantic Serra do Marão into the *Amarante* 40 km to the west with its old Tâmega Bridge.

CASTELO BRANCO

(110/B1) Even though little remains of the old 13th century ⁐ Templar Castle from which the town takes its name ("white castle"), nevertheless it still offers a wide view of the town and the olive groves which surround it. Situated near to the border, during times of unrest this town (Pop. c.45,000) was obliged to defend itself against its enemies with the help of its massive defensive walls. Today the best olive oil in the whole of Portugal is pressed in Castel Branco.

SIGHTS

Jardim Episcopal

When experts on the country describe these baroque gardens as the most beautiful in Portugal they are not exaggerating. Formerly the Bishop's gardens, they are certainly some of the loveli-

Rural scenes such as this can still be seen in the hills of northern Portugal

Portuguese and Spanish kings line the staircase in Portugal's most beautiful gardens

implements. The collection of paintings with Portuguese pictures from the 16th to the 20th centuries is of interest. However, we recommend the beautiful colcha embroidery (artistically worked bedspreads or tablecloths, but which are best used as wall-coverings in view of their value) which is typical of Castelo Branco. Only the museum continues to safeguard the tradition of this embroidery. Mainly floral motifs but also portrayals of people and animals are worked on natural-coloured linen. *Open daily 10 am–midday and 2.30–5 pm, admission $ 400, Rua Frei Bartolomeu da Costa*

est in Portugal. It is not just the artistic topiaries. the daintily laid out beds and ponds that have made the gardens famous, but also and especially the many statues which adorn the terraced landscape. The highlight is the flight of stone steps with statues of a complete series of Portuguese kings. Although there are disputes as to which particular attribute is characteristic of which king, there is one thing that all Portuguese agree about, namely, that the Spanish Hapsburg kings are quite rightly shown as smaller than their Portuguese predecessors and successors. *Open daily except public holidays 9 am to sunset, admission $ 50, Rua Frei Bartolomeu da Costa*

MUSEUM

Museu de Francisco Tavares Proença Júnior

★ In its lower rooms the museum houses pre- and early historical finds from the surrounding area. The upper floor displays agricultural and domestic

RESTAURANTS

We recommend giving preference to the traditional cuisine of the region, especially lamb dishes. Of course you should also try the famous cheese from Alcains and from the Serra which goes so well even with the sweet wines from Hermínio and Cavaca.

Arcadia

◈ A good restaurant favoured by the locals for its selection of regional specialities. *Rua Sídonio Pais, Tel. 272/219 33, Category 3*

Praça Velha

The best restaurant in town. *Praça Luís de Camìes, Tel. 272/32 86 40, Category 2*

ACCOMMODATION

Pensão Arraiana

This well-run guest house has 31 rooms with baths, *Av. 1° de Maio 18, Tel. 272/34 16 34, Fax 33 88 14, Category 3*

Hotel Colina do Castelo

Belonging to the Meliá Group, this hotel has a swimming pool and tennis courts and is perhaps the most beautiful house in the town. *103 rooms, Rua da Piscina, Tel. 272/32 98 56, Fax 32 97 59, Category 2*

Hotel Rainha D. Amélia

A new hotel, suitable for the disabled and with its own restaurant. *64 rooms, Rua de Santiago 15, Tel. 272/32 63 15, Fax 32 63 90, Category 2*

ENTERTAINMENT

For evening entertainment you can visit one of the many bars, for example *O Património*, or go dancing in the discotheque ⚐ *A Alternativa* or *República (8 km outside the town on the N 112 in the Salgueiro direction)*.

INFORMATION

Turismo

Alameda da Liberdade, Tel. 272/210 02, Fax 33 03 24

SURROUNDING AREA

Barragem da Idanha   (106/A 6)

About 50 km north-east of Castelo Branco the waters of the Rio Ponsul are dammed in the Barragem da Idanha. The leisure value of this artifical lake is so high because here visitors can enjoy the solitude of nature well away from the bustle of tourists.

Idanha-a-Velha   (106/B 6)

Some 15 km from the Idanha reservoir lies Idanha-a-Velha, today deserted, once the large Roman settlement of Civitas

Egaetidanis and in Early Christian times the episcopal seat Egitania. It sank into obscurity following the Moorish invasion. The village *church*, built on the foundations of a Roman temple, houses a collection of finds from the Roman and Visigoth era. The key to the church must be obtained from the verger.

Monsanto   (106/B 6)

〰 From the castle mound with the remains of walls and fortress ruins there is a fine view over the countryside and the village below. The grey granite houses lean up against the rock, sometimes they are even set vertically into the stone.

When walking along the uneven pavements through the village the visitor will be impressed by the fact that even in this stony desert people have not lost their sense of beauty. Simple Manueline shapes adorn the door and window frames, colourful flowers on window sills and in front gardens make this remote village a truly idyllic spot.

GUARDA

(106/A 3) In this, the highest town in Portugal (Pop. c.25,000), everything appears geared to defence and protection: the former fortifications and even the Sé (cathedral). From the 〰 *Torre de Menagem* there is a view over the whole town. Even when you enter the *Misericórdia church* with its excessively ornate baroque decoration or wander through the market (1st and 3rd Wednesdays in the month) you will detect that even in the midst of bare rock and cold fortifications the sense of beauty and sheer joy of living remains.

Sé (Cathedral)
A mixture of Gothic, Renaissance and baroque styles. The fortified exterior is in interesting contrast to the Manueline interior. ◁▷ Visitors can climb up into the rafters.

RESTAURANTS

There are several restaurants in the *Rua Francisco de Passar*. Specially recommended: *O Reduto (Category 3)*

Restaurante O Telheiro
✪ Speciality restaurant. Simply must be tried: the local mountain cheese *queijo da serra*. *Estrada Nacional 16, Tel. 271/21 13 56, Category 2*

ACCOMMODATION

Pensão Pinto
Simply furnished, a few kilometres north-east in Pombeira-Arrifana. *17 rooms, Tel. 271/23 92 20, Fax 23 95 18, Category 3*

Solar de Alarcão
A manor house in the centre of the historic quarter. *3 rooms, Rua D. Miguel de Alarcao 25, Tel. 271/21 43 92, Fax 21 12 75, Category 2*

Hotel Turismo da Guarda
Middle class hotel, elegantly furnished, with a night-club, swimming pool and park complex. *106 rooms, Av. Coronel Orlindo de Carvalho, Tel. 271/22 33 66, Fax 22 33 99, Category 1–2*

INFORMATION

Turismo
Praça Luís de Camões, Tel. 271/22 33 66, Fax 22 33 99

SURROUNDING AREA

Serra da Estrela (105/F 4, 106/A 4)
★ A mountain tour through the little towns of Belmonte and Manteigas and in the Serra de Estrela National Park offers everything the nature lover could desire: bizarre rock formations, deep ravines, wild brooks, shady woods, wide views and refreshing mountain air.

Vila Nova de Foz Côa (106/A 1)
To the north of Guarda not far from the Spanish border there is an *open air archaeological park* along the river with cave paintings.

VISEU

(105/E 3) The old provincial town of Viseu (Pop. 22,500) is worth a visit because it has retained its rural charm: there are some lovely walks across old squares and through narrow lanes, e.g. the Direita shopping street. Also it was here that the major Portuguese painter Vasco Fernandes, known as Grão Vasco, founded Viseu's legendary school of painting.

SIGHTS

Sé (Cathedral)
This 13th century church has been remodelled again and again. This is seen clearly on the different towers (dating from the 13th and 17th centuries). Particularly

worth seeing is the two-storeyed cloister. *Praça da Sé*

Museu Grão Vasca

★ The museum – named after the town's most renowned son (1480–1543) – is housed in the former bishops' palace; note the passionate naturalism and unique use of colours by Grao Vasco. *Open Tue–Sun 9.30 am–12.30 pm and 2–5.30 pm, admission $ 250, Praça da Sé*

Cortiço

Good cuisine, beautiful ambience. *Rua do Hilário, Tel. 232/42 38 53, Category 2*

Trave Negra

☺ Regional speciality dishes. Personally tipped by the locals. *Rua dos Loureiros 40, Tel. 232/261 38, Category 2*

Hotel Grão Vasco

Reputedly the best hotel in town. *111 rooms, Rua Gaspar Barreiros, Tel. 232/42 35 11, Fax 42 64 44, Category 1–2*

Hotel Príncipe Perfeito

Former manor house in Cabanões, about 4 km south of the town. *43 rooms, Tel. 232/46 92 00, Fax 46 92 10, Category 2*

Viseu has a lot of bars. Young people meet in the ⚸ *Metrópolis*; it is quieter in the *Chaplin*. Popular fado spot: *Retiro do Hilário*.

Turismo

Av. Gulbenkian, Tel. 232/42 20 14, Fax 42 18 64

Lamego   (101/E 6)

★ In the heart of the port wine region on the banks of the Douro lies the old episcopal town of Lamego with its beautiful *cathedral*, interesting *regional museum* and the 7th century Visigoth church of *São Pedro de Balsemão* (3 km outside the town). Particularly interesting is the pilgrimage church of *Nossa Senhora dos Remédios* (cloister with 14 stations of the cross; almost 200 steps).

There is some charming scenery to be seen along the winding road from Lamego northwards through the port wine region to Régua and Vila Real.

Régua   (101/E 6)

Régua, officially Peso da Régua, lies in the middle of the portwine region. in the *Turismo (Rua da Ferreirinha, Tel./Fax 254/31 28 46)* there are maps obtainable with all 54 *quintas* (vineyards) in the region which produce port wine and are open to visitors. Accommodation in Régua in the feudal manor house *Casa das Torres de Oliveira (six rooms, Tel. 254/33 67 43, Fax 33 61 95, Category 1)* or in Pinhão 25 km to the west: In the centre of the vineyards with a view of the Douro visitors can stay in the *Hotel Vintage House (40 rooms, Tel. 254/73 02 30, Fax 73 02 38, Category 1).*

Castles, monasteries, Roman ruins

On the road between Porto (Oporto) and Lisbon relics of the past are lined up like a string of pearls

The Beira Litoral, as the coastal province between Douro and the countryside surrounding Lisbon was once named, is a region full of contrasts. The long, white sandy beaches were once covered by green pine-forests; in recent years more and more eucalyptus plantations have been established. Silt deposits have created a 6,000 ha lagoon (Ria de Aveiro) on the River Vouga. Here the gaudily coloured fishing boats lay at anchor. White mountains of salt are piled up in front of the salt-works and visitors can sample oysters at large breeding stations. In the hinterland rice, maize, wheat and vegetables are grown in the fertile soil. However, income is often insufficient to support a family, and so many small farmers seek secondary employment in the

Nets have to be mended: fishermen at work on Nazaré beach

industrial firms which have become established along the main road between Oporto and Lisbon. Portugal's history can be studied in the immediate vicinity of this main traffic artery: the Roman era in Conimbriga, the history of education in the university town of Coimbra, Portuguese pride and sense of history in Batalha, convents in Alcobaça, the Order of the Knights of Christ in Tomar and (commercialized) piety in Fátima.

AVEIRO

(104/B 3) By means of its silt deposits the Rio Vouga has created a wall against the sea behind which stretches the 40 km long and 10 km wide Ria de Aveiro. Aveiro itself (Pop. c.30,000) lies at the southern end of the lagoon, and ships can pass from the harbour to the open sea only through a narrow channel. The

51

town, with its flooded streets making it the Vienna of Portugal, lives on fishing and salt-production. An ambitious new harbour is currently being built because, as a member of the EU, Aveiro dreams of becoming a world port which could also ship all over the world Spanish goods brought into Portugal by land. Until then, however, much river and sea water still mixes in the Ria on which the *moliceira* in their long, narrow boats with the uniquely curved and painted bows still do as they have always done and collect seaweed with which to fertilize the already fertile soil of the region.

SIGHTS

Old Town

The starting point for a walk through the Old Town is the *Praça da República* with the *town hall* and *Church of the Misericórdia* (beautiful 16th century Renaissance doorway). Further on is the 15th century *Sé* (cathedral) with its baroque façade (1719). Inside is a rare wooden statue of the Virgin Mary and the tomb of Caterina de Attayde, the mistress of the poet Camões. In front of the church stands a particularly beautiful wayside cross, the *Cruzeiro de São Domingos*. It is worth making a trip to the *railway station* in the east of the town, at the end of Avenida Dr. Lourenço Peixinho, in order to see the painted tiles *azulejos*.

MUSEUM

Museu Regional

Here, in the former Convent of Jesus, the king's daughter Joana lived as a simple nun until she died in 1490 aged thirty-eight. In beatific terms she is revered as a saint. As well as her tomb the following are of interest: art gallery, ecclesiastical art, as well as the boots and equipment of the *moliceiros* (fishers of seaweed). In the convent church can be seen some exuberant *talha* and *azulejo* work.*Open Tue–Sun 10 am–12.30 pm and 2–5 pm, admission $ 350, Rua de S. Joana*

RESTAURANTS

Sea and river decide what appears on the table in Aveiro. Things viewed as specialities elsewhere are on every menu here: mussels on a skewer, crustaceans, fish soup with eel, marinated eel, as well as braised lamb, roast sucking pig, candied eggs *(ovos moles)*. The ultimate, however, is a *caldeirada*, a fish stew. Those who like a change should try the *verde* wine in preference to a strong Dão wine.

Restaurant Imperial

A good restaurant in the hotel of the same name, also with local cuisine. *Rua Dr. Nascimento Leitão, Tel. 234/221 41, Category 2*

ACCOMMODATION

Residencial Alboi

A good hotel situated in the town centre. *22 rooms, Rua da Arrochela 6, Tel. 234/251 21, Fax 220 63, Category 2–3*

Hotel As Américas

Four-star hotel in the centre. *70 rooms, Rua Engenheiro Von Hafe 20, Tel. 234/38 46 40, Fax 38 42 58, Category 1–2*

INFORMATION

Turismo
Rua João Mendonça 8, Tel. 234/236 80, Fax 283 26

SURROUNDING AREA

Arouca (105/D 2)
★ A day trip inland to the north is rewarding. From Aveiro via Ovar and São da Medeira the N 327 and N 326 minor roads passing through lovely mountain countryside take you to Arouca. The effort will be rewarded when you visit the Romanesque *convent* with its baroque interior and the *museum* with valuable paintings by Portuguese artists. From here continue further to the Misarela *waterfall* and then follow the N 326 to the *Monte da Senhora da Mó*

Ria (104/B 2–3)
A boat trip on the Ria, past salt-mountains and drying plant, is an interesting experience. *Example of cost: trip from Aveiro to Torreira and back from $ 2000*

Buçaco Forest (104/C 4)
Drive by way of Ílhavo (**104/B 3**) to *Vista Alegre* (8 km), where purchases can be made in the *porcelain museum* which gives an insight into the long tradition of porcelain manufacture. Those with children or who themselves like water sports should make a detour to *Barra* and *Costa Nova* (**104/B 3**). If you wish you can make a further detour to *Figueira da Foz* (**104/B 5**), the chic bathing resort at the mouth of the Mondego (casino, gala evenings, azulejo splendour).

Then proceed via the spa town of *Curia* to the Buçaco Forest near *Luso*. In this large forest, where women have for a long time not dared to venture, more than 700 different species of plants can be studied. Visitors can also stay in the summer palace built by King Carlos in 1887 and which today is a *luxury hotel (Palace Hotel, 64 rooms, Buçaco/Mealhada, Tel. 231/93 01 01/02/03, Fax 93 05 09, category 1).* Those not wishing to stay the night should at least see the

MARCO POLO SELECTION: COSTA DE PRATA

former *palace* built in the Manueline style and enjoy lunch in the large dining room.

COIMBRA

(104/C 5) The saying goes in Portugal that people pray in Braga, work in Oporto, live in Lisbon and study in Coimbra (Pop. c.100,000). From ⚕ University Square in front of the famous library containing more than 120,000 volumes there is a fine view of the Mondego Valley and the Santa Clara convent. Not only professors and students have their say up here; it is said that all spiritual and political movements and trends which have ever changed Portugal would have had their origins here. Student customs, such as the wearing of ribbons and the *capa preta* (black capes), the *queima das fitas* (burning of the ribbons on completion of their studies in May) and the fado are felt in student quarters *repúblicas* to be their duty to the spiritual elite.

A stroll through the little shopping lanes around the Praça do Comércio will also be found rewarding.

SIGHTS

Churches
The *Sé Velha* is the largest cathedral in Portugal. a three-storeyed building with a Late Gothic altar (portrayal of the Assumption of the Virgin Mary). The first king of Portugal. Alfonso Henrique, lies buried in the *Igreja Santa Cruz* (worth a visit to see the fine *azulejos*). The Igreja *Santa-Clara-a-Velha*, which slowly sank into the mud of the river during past centuries, is now being raised.

Quinta das Lágrimas
In this "Garden of Tears" Portugal's most passionate love story came to a tragic end: Inês, the sweetheart of Crown Prince Pedro, was murdered in the beautiful park belonging to the mansion house (now a hotel). See Route 2, page 89. After walking through the park enjoy a drink by the open fire in the feudal hotel. *At the south-western exit from the town, near the N 1.*

University library
★ Modelled on the Court Library in Vienna, there are theological and philosophical books in the green room, scientific ones in the red room and antique works in the black room. Everything that has been thoughtfully acquired in Portugal from the Middle Ages to the present day is housed in these magnificent rooms. Before leaving the university by passing the clock tower and going out through the *porta ferrea* (iron door), have a look in the university church with its Manueline doorway and beautiful *azulejos* inside. *Open Tue–Sun 10 am–midday and 2–5 pm, admission $ 250 to library only, $ 500 to the church, museum and library.*

MUSEUM

Museu Machado de Castro
A noble building (portal, galleries, inner courtyard with fountain). The lower floor houses mainly Romanesque, Gothic and Manueline sculptures, the ⚕ upper floor (superb view} gold and silversmith work. Especially beautiful are the items in the Rainha

Santa Room. *Open Tue–Sun 9.30 am–5.30 pm, Admission $ 250, Largo Dr. José Rodrigues*

RESTAURANTS/CAFÉ

Specialities of the town include rice with lamprey *à moda do Vale do Mondego* and *chanfana* (kid roasted in wine) as well as Santa Clara pies for dessert.

Café Santa Cruz

The finest coffee house is in the cloister vaults of the church of the same name.

Trovador

A fine establishment, fado at weekends. *Largo da Sé Velha 15, Tel. 239/254 75, Category 1–2*

Zé Manel dos Ossos

❂ Typical restaurant. *Beco do Forno, Tel. 239/237 90, Category 3*

ACCOMMODATION

Hotel D. Luís

❂ Opposite Coimbra with a fine view of the town. *104 rooms, Quinta da Varzea, Tel. 239/44 25 10, Fax 44 51 96, Category 2*

Quinta das Lágrimas

Portugal's most stylish manor house. Kings and army commanders have stayed here; a refuge from walking in the footsteps of Pedro and Inês, Portugal's most famous lovers. *39 rooms, Tel. 239/44 16 15, Fax 44 16 95, Category 1*

ENTERTAINMENT

Evenings in Coimbra should be devoted to the fado: the best place to go is the *Diligência Bar*

(Rua Nova 30). Young people favour the ⚡ *Scotch* discotheque and the *Via Latina* or *Galeria Almedina* bars. Pubs and piano bars can be found around the cathedral.

INFORMATION

Turismo
Largo da Portagem, Tel. 239/82 04 01, Fax 255 76

SURROUNDING AREA

Conimbriga **(104/C 6)**
★ An extensive well preserved Roman town ruins. Originally founded by the Celts, it was an important Roman base between Lisbon and Oporto. Visitors will be able to gain an impression of the size, wealth and beauty of the town. The museum adjoining the site is also worth a visit. Material recovered from the excavations is on display. *Open Tue–Sun 10 am–6 pm, admission $ 350*

A Roman mosaic floor in the town ruins at Conimbriga

There is a beautiful drive through the Mondego Valley to *Penacova* past windmills above the town and into the Buçaco Forest.

NAZARÉ

(108/B-C 2) Deeply suntanned men sit on the little beach wall mending their nets. Two old men observe the throng of tourists. Their skin is leathery, they wear woollen hats or sailors' caps, fishermen's smocks and seamen's jackets. There is no mistake about it, Nazaré lives from fishing. Even though the boats are no longer pulled out of the water by ox-carts in the traditional way – Nazaré (Pop. c.16,000) has had a modern harbour basin for a few years now – the little town still has all the charm of a fishing port; brightly coloured washing hangs over the narrow white lanes and many fisherwomen still wear the short wide skirts typical of Nazaré. Moreover the town has one of the prettiest beaches in Portugal.

SIGHTS

São Miguel
◁▷ Lighthouse and fortress on the cliffs. A walk to the top of the cliffs is worth the effort!

Sítio
◁▷ This is the name of that part of the town on the 100 m high cliffs. You can climb up along the footpath, take the cable railway (41 per cent gradient) for $ 105 or drive to the top by car. At the viewing-point stands the tiny *Capela da Memória*, which is richly decorated with *azulejos*. Nearby stands the column with the Cross of the Knights of Christ. The inscription says that Vasco da Gama came here after his voyage to India to give thanks to the Virgin of Nazaré for his safe return. In the small *museum* archaeological finds are displayed together with depictions of a fisherman's life.

HOTELS/RESTAURANTS

In summer nearly every house rents out a room; the *Europe, Ideal* and *Leonardo* guest houses are good value.

Albergaria Mar Bravo
Close to the sea with restaurant. *16 rooms, Praça Sousa Oliveira 67, Tel. 262/55 10 92, Fax 55 39 79, Category 1*

Pensão Ribamar
Creaking floorboards, rooms with open fires, good food, very close to the beach. *23 rooms, Rua Gomes Freire 9, Tel. 262/55 11 58, Fax 56 22 24, Category 2*

ENTERTAINMENT

Nazaré has a ✸ *cinema*; next to the cinema the *folk music groups* "Tamar" and "Mar Alto" appear on alternate evenings in summer from 10 pm onwards. After eating, people meet in the *Pena Branca Bar* or in the ✪ *Fora d'horas* disco.
7 km south of Nazaré lies Famalicão. In the ✪ *O Marquês* bar there is fado singing at the weekend from 10 pm.

INFORMATION

Turismo
Av. da República, Tel. 262/56 11 94, Fax 550 10 49

SURROUNDING AREA

Alcobaça (108/C 2)

Alcobaça is a sleepy little town with a pretty *wine museum (admission free)* and some good restaurants, such as the *Celeira dos Frades,* the decor of which is redolent of a convent hall *(Av. de Cister, tel. 262/422 81, Category 2).*

However, nobody would suspect that here on the main square of Alcobaça (Pop. c.5,500) stands the largest sacred building in Portugal: a *Cistercian abbey (open daily 9 am–5 pm, until 7 pm in summer, admission $ 400)* with a cathedral dating back to the 12th/13th centuries. Scarcely 20 m wide but more than 100 m long, the nave appears cold and plain. The only decorations are on the sarcophagi of the country's most famous lovers, Dona Inês and Prince Pedro. Although the prince was married to the Spanish Princess of Castile he fell in love with her lady-in-waiting Inês de Castro. After the death of his wife he married Inês but soon afterwards his father had her murdered. After the death of his father Prince Pedro had his sweetheart's body exhumed and taken to Alcobaça where she was crowned as queen. The sarcophagus of Inês is supported by crouching animal figures representing her murderers. The other coffin is adorned with a portrayal of Christ's Passion. The sarcophagi of the two lovers are placed foot to foot so that when they arise on the Day of Judgement they will look at once into each others' eyes. A further item of interest in the monastery complex is the *monastery kitchen* where meals are prepared for a thousand monks every day. Under the 20 m tall chimney hood several oxen can be roasted at the same time.

Visitors can stay in an elegant renovated manor house not far from the town centre: *Chalet Fonte Nova, 6 rooms, Estrada da Fonte Nova, Tel. 262/59 65 96, Fax 59 84 30, Category 1*

Batalha (108/C 2)

The most impressive view of the Batalha Abbey complex is obtained when you approach Batalha (Pop. c.8,000) from Leira. i.e. from the north. Suddenly there it is: massive, majestic, magnificent. The building can attribute its existence to the winning of a battle. In 1385, when the Portuguese army faced a superior Spanish force, the Portuguese king promised to build an abbey if they won. It took two hundred years to build this "greatest abbey of all time" and the architectural forms range from High Gothic via the Manueline style to the Renaissance. The church nave is 80 m long and 32 m high. The most beautiful part of the building is the cloister *(admission $ 500),* the *Claustro Real,* with its magnificently decorated window-arches, a Manueline showpiece. The *equestrian statue* in front of the abbey portrays the royal commander who led the Portuguese to victory over the Spaniards. There is a folk festival here on 14 August every year commemorating the battle.

Grutas de Santo António (109/D 2)
20 km from Alcobaça, in the direction of Porto de Mós, lie the most impressive caves in Portugal, the Grutas de Santo António and Grutas de Alvados. The caves are huge (total area 6,000 sq m) and full of fantastic scenery – from impressive underground lakes to fairytale stone forests – , all skilfully illuminated. A rewarding excursion. *Open daily 9.30 am–6 pm, until 8 pm in summer, admission $ 500 per cave.*

Leiria **(108/C 1–2)**
On the left bank of the River Liz lies the regional capital Leira (Pop. c.30,000). It is a busy market town in the centre of the country. From the castle-★ ☙ keep there is a fine view out into the countryside and of the *Pinhal de Leira*, one of the largest pine forests in Portugal. You should also visit the *loggia* of the former royal palace with its slender Gothic columns and three-aisled cathedral in the Renaissance style. If you have time visit one of the town's many museums: the *art gallery*, the *local museum*, the *school museum* or Sporting Club's *museum of sport*.

Óbidos **(108/B 3)**
Óbidos (Pop. 1000) is probably the prettiest and most attractive little town in Portugal: with its picturesque little lanes and old encircling wall it is a must for any tourist. Most stay only a few hours and glance briefly in the church of *Santa Maria*, the chapel of *São Martinho* and the small museum. On the 13 m high ☙ walls visitors can walk once round the town in less than an hour and look down on the whitewashed houses with

their windows decorated with flowers. It really merits a longer visit in order to see the interesting corners and alleyways as well as the many Baroque and Renaissance houses.

Anyone staying in the *pousada* in Óbidos *(9 rooms, Paço Real, Tel. 262/95 91 05, Fax 95 91 48, Category 1)* should treat themselves to one of the rooms in the tower. Reserve a room in good time in the summer! At Easter an impressive procession passes through the whole town.

TOMAR

(109/E 2) The town lies in the fertile Ribatejo countryside near a dam with an adjoining recreation area. After first leaving behind you the new buildings at the entrance to the town you will again find yourself in a pretty little community (Pop. c.15,000): a picturesque river, the Nabão, a tributary of the Tejo, with weeping willows and ivy-covered café terraces, a beautiful park, churches of all kinds and a massive castle complex on the hill overlooking the town.

SIGHTS

Convent-Castle of the Knights of Christ
☙ The town is dominated by the majestic castle. It is one of the country's really great sights and has been declared a Cultural Heritage Site by UNESCO. The former seat of two orders of knights – first the Order of Templars, later the Order of the Knights of Christ – was continually extended over a period of five centuries. It consists of two

The Pearl of the Atlantic

A proud and confident capital city and chic living in the old seaside resorts

Lisbon, capital of Portugal, lies on a massive natural harbour less than 20 kilometres from the Atlantic Ocean on the north bank of the Tejo (Tagus). The climate is mild, there are many thermal springs, and subtropical forests grow inland. To the west of Lisbon stretches Portugal's Côte d'Azur; kings and millionaires once used to spend the autumn here – in picturesque fairy-tale castles on the outskirts of pretty fishing villages. Over the years, however, the tiny villages have grown into chic tourist centres with huge hotel complexes and golf courses. Idyllic peace is a thing of the past. The towns have long since merged into cities.

LISBON (LISBOA)

☛ **Plan of the city inside back cover**

(112/B 2) Oppressive heat, sticky atmosphere, loud car horns, busy traffic; the cafés are full to over-crowding, people are reading

The Monument of the Discoveries: at the head of a throng of explorers, cartographers and sailors stands their patron Henry the Navigator

newspapers, discussing events or enjoying the hustle and bustle on the Rossio, Lisbon's best-known square.

Or you can go up to the Chiado, the district with many cafés and boutiques which is named after the pseudonym of the poet Ribeiro. He smiles down from a memorial statue near the old Café A Brasileira. You have a choice: either wander wearily through the little lanes leading up to the Bairro Alto or choose the easier route and for $ 160 take the Elevador de Santa Justa, a great iron lift dating from 1901 (with a café on the viewing platform) up to the quarter which is home to goldsmiths, antique dealers, artists, with pubs and taverns where the fado is sung in the evenings. Then just wander up and down through the narrow little lanes.

In 1755 a serious earthquake caused much devastation and destroyed almost the whole city. Only a few districts escaped unscathed. The lower part of the city was rebuilt under the direction of the Marquês de Pombal on strict geometric lines linking the ★ Rossio and Praça do Comércio squares. The former

King and Market Square is actually almost perfectly square in shape with government buildings on three sides. Marble steps lead down to the river. At one time returning seafarers were welcomed here. There is, however, another Lisbon, a highly modern one. Expo 98, the last World Exhibition of the 20th century, changed the face of the city: more than three billion pounds sterling was spent on building bridges, railway stations, underground railways and the Expo site. Many housing complexes were completed or sensitively redeveloped – thanks to the initiative of the mayor Joao Soares, the son of a former state president, who devoted himself to rebuilding those quarters of Lisbon rich in tradition in a manner as true to the originals as possible. The most outstanding development is that near the river. For centuries Lisbon had been cut off from the Tejo (Tagus) by warehouses and walls. Now there are more and more green open spaces, places where people can stroll and also popular meeting spots. This is where it all happens in the Lisbon of today (Pop. 1,000,000, nearly 3,000,000 in Greater Lisbon).

If you have only a short time in Lisbon, you should at least visit the Rossio, the true heart of the city, and go out to Belém.

SIGHTS

Alfama (U/E 4–5)

✪ Alfama calls itself Lisbon's oldest district and it escaped largely unscathed in the earthquake. Here it is best not to follow a fixed plan but simply to take plenty of time to stroll at leisure through the narrow lanes and little stepped streets where

---

MARCO POLO SELECTION: LISBON

1 Cristo Rei
From the statue of Christ on the south bank of the Tejo (Tagus) there is a superb view of Lisbon (page 63)

2 Rossio and Santa Luzia
A walk from the Rossio, the main square, down through the Rua do Ouro to the Tejo (Tagus). At the Praça do Comércio proceed east past the cathedral to the Santa Luzia viewing terrace; a good view of the Old Town (Alfama) and the river (pages 61 and 63)

3 Belém
The district by the Tejo (Tagus) with buildings from the age of discovery (page 63)

4 Oceanarium
Europe's largest aquarium (page 64)

5 Cabo da Roca
Buffeted by winds and Europe's most westerly point (page 69)

6 Sintra
Wherever you go you will meet up with the past – a little town just made for strolling and lingering (page 68)

the fado is said to have originated, past romantic open courtyards and wall arches.

As a starting-out point for a stroll through Alfama you should choose either the ★ ◁ *Miradouro de Santa Luzia* or ◁ *Castelo de São Jorge,* the city's finest viewing point. Until the 16th century the latter was the royal residence but it was largely destroyed in the Lisbon earthquake. Today the castle complex is mainly a popular spot with courting couples and tourists. Built into the walls is the *Casa do Leão* restaurant *(Tel. 21/887 59 62, Category 1; fado music on Tue, Thu, Fri from 10.30 pm).*

Belém (O)

★ An old quarter 7 km west of the city centre. On the bank of the Tejo (Tagus) stand buildings redolent of the golden age of discovery, as well as some of the city's major sights: the Jerónimos Monastery, the modern seafaring monument the Padrao dos Descobrimentos, the very the symbol of Lisbon, the ◁ *Torre de Belém (Open Tue–Sun 10 am–5 pm, admission $ 400).* This elaborate 16th century fortified lighthouse built in the Manueline style once stood on an island and served as a defensive bulwark at the harbour entrance. As a result of the silting up of the river it is now on the river bank. For a time it was also used as a prison by by the Spanish conquerors. In 1807 French troops destroyed the top two storeys which were later rebuilt.

Visitors can see the dungeons and climb up to the 35 m high platform. Visible from the Torre de Belém, by the marina, the proud ◁ Monument of the Discoveries *(Padrão dos Descobrimentos)* stands 52 m high. It was erected in 1960 to commemorate the 500th anniversary of the death of Henry the Navigator. In the prow of a ship stand larger-than-life Portuguese explorers, navigators, cartographers, seamen, artists and missionaries. A lift *$ 400* will take visitors up to the top of the monument. As well as a view of the Cristo Rei statue this also gives the best view over the city.

The interesting Mosteiro dos Jerónimos (Jerónimos Monastery) is a prime example of Manueline architecture. King Manuel I commissioned it at the end of the 15th century as a token of thanks for Vasco da Gama's successful voyage to India, but it finally took fifty years to complete. It has a magnificent *south door* and inside is the *tomb of Vasco da Gama,* who discovered India. The *cloister* which adjoins the church to the north is regarded by many as the most beautiful in Portugal.

In the *Centro Cultural da Belém,* the country's largest cultural centre, a visit to the *Design Museum* is worthwhile. A stone's throw from the Jerónimos Monastery, in the Rua Veira Portuense, lie the *Cais de Belém,* a veritable glutton's delight. In the Rua de Belém you should definitely visit the *Antiga Confeitaria de Belém,* a 160 year-old coffee house with a pastry maker's shop.

Cristo Rei (O)

★ ◁ On the other side of the city stands the Cristo Rei, a statue of Christ with arms outstretched safeguarding the city, visible from the centre of Lisbon.

Like so many of Portugal's monuments, this one was also built to fulfil a vow: it was erected in 1959 as a token of gratitude that Portugal had not been involved in the Second World War. There is a chapel built into the 82 m high base. A lift goes up to the terrace at the foot of the 28 m tall statue. From here there is a magnificent view of Lisbon. *Open daily 9 am–6.30 pm, admission $ 250*

Alcântara Docks/ Cais do Sodré   (U/A 5-6, O)

Recently a number of promenades have appeared along the Tejo (Tagus). The *Esplanada da Doca de Santos* is Lisbon's "in" street for eating and drinking and entertainment: cafés, bar-restaurants and discotheques in the former harbour buildings close to the marina. At the *Cais do Sodré* it is worth visiting the *Portugália, a traditional brewery* or *Armazém F*, where you draw your own beer.

Expo sites and Oceanarium   (O)

"Park of Nations" (Parque das Nações) is the name given to the 330 hectare former exhibition site with its fair pavilions, marinas, museums and theatre halls, gardens, a railway station and Europe's largest ★ *Oceanarium (Open daily 10 am–7 pm, admission $ 2,000)*. In the years to come a new city quarter with offices, shops and houses will be developed here.

Also of interest is the new *Oriente underground station*, a complete work of art including sculptures, large-format *azulejo* pictures and designer furniture.

The Catalan architect Santiago Calatrava, the Icelandic pop artist Errî, the Portuguese Joaquim Rodrigo and the Austrian Friedensreich Hundertwasser all contributed. You can find the murals in all the underground stations on the internet under *www.metrolisboa,pt.*

Palácia Fronteira   (O)

In the 17th century this palace and gardens in the suburb of Benfica was regarded as the eighth wonder of the world. *Mon–Sat 10.30 am–midday there are guided tours every half an hour (at 11 am and midday only in winter), admission to palace $ 1500, garden $ 500, Largo São Domingos de Benfica*

Parque de Eduardo VII   (U/B-C 1)

◁▷ One of Lisbon's best known views is that over the city and down to the Tejo from high up in the large park called Parque de Eduardo VII. Below the park lies the large square known as Parque Marquês de Pombal. From it leads the *Avenida da Liberdade*, the palm-lined boulevard with eight traffic lanes, ten rows of trees and six pavements, most of them artistically paved with mosaics

Ponte de 25 de Abril and Ponte Vasco da Gama   (O)

Superlative bridges: one (the 25 de Abril) is Europe's longest suspension bridge (70 m high, 3 km long); since 1999 it has also carried trains. The other (Vasco da Gama) is Europe's longest bridge; almost 18 kilometres long it spans the eastern bay of the Tejo.

Sé (Cathedral)   (U/E 5)
A little way below the ◀▶ Santa Luzia square stands the mighty cathedral dating from 1147. It is the city's oldest edifice and has a fortress-like appearance.

Tram ride
◆ It is worthwhile taking a ride on a tram (*e.g. line 28, $ 150*). In summer two 1901 trams are brought into service just for tours of the city; *Linha das Colinas* (hill trip): tour through the Old Town, *Linha do Tejo* (Tagus trip): goes along the banks of the river to the sights in Belém. *Departure from the Terreiro do Paço* (**U/D 5**), as the Praça do Comércio is known in Lisbon. *Adults $ 4,900, children $ 1,500*

MUSEUMS

Europe's 1994 city of culture possesses a great many museums and galleries. There are maritime, fado and railway museums, a children's museum, a radio museum, one for the theatre and music, even a water museum and a pastry museum. Likewise underground railway stops have been made into small museums. Those wishing for information in advance can obtain details from the internet (*www.ipmuseus.pt*).

Museu Calouste Gulbenkian   (O)
Established by an oil magnate. Antique works of art and other items are on display. (*Open Tue–Sun 10 am–5 pm, admission $ 500, Av. de Berna 45*

Museu Nacional de Arte Antiga   (U/A 5)
The city's major museum. Ceramics, tapestries, worked gold articles, important art gallery. *Open Wed–Sun 10 am–2 pm, Tue 2–6 pm, admission $ 500, Rua das Janelas Verdes 9*

Museu Nacional do Azulejo   (O)
Collection of *azulejos* dating from their introduction until the present day. *Open Wed–Sun 10 am–6 pm, Tue 2–6 pm, admission $ 350,*

Tours of the town by tram start from the Praça do Comércio

Sun 10 am–2 pm admission free, Rua Madre de Deus 4

Museu Nacional dos Coches (O)

60 magnificent coaches from the 16th to 19th centuries and well worth seeing. *Open Tue–Sun 10 am–5.30 pm, admission $ 500, on the Parque dos Naáoes Expo site*

RESTAURANTS

Lisbon's "food mile" starts at the Rossio near the Teatro Nacional *(Rua das Portas de santo Antão).* Those who prefer more down-to-earth places can try the *Rua de São Miguel* in Alfama, a street of tiny taverns. The *Bairro Alto* is more intellectual; the scenic quarter by the docks close to the Tejo has a Mediterranean feel.

Alcântara Café (O)

A must for those who like something special: in a former factory, with plastic and plush decor. *Rua Maria Luísa Holstein 15, Tel. 21/362 12 26, Category 1–2*

Bota Alta (U/C 4)

A cosy meeting place for artists. *Travessa Queimada 27, Tel. 21/342 79 59, Category 1*

Café In (O)

Large fish selection. *Av. de Brasília, Pavilhão Nascente, tel. 21/362 62 49, Category 1*

Cervejaria Trindade (U/D 5)

The vaulted cloister decorated with *azulejos* resembles a railway station. Good beer, reasonably priced meals. *Rua Nova da Trindade 20, Tel. 21/342 35 06, Category 2–3*

Doca Seis (O)

At the docks you are spoiled for choice with the many eating places. Here you get value for money as well as atmosphere. *Doca de Santo Amaro, Tel. 21/395 79 05, Category 1–2*

Pap'Açorda (U/C 4)

For intellectuals, lots of marble. *Rua da Atalaia 57, Tel. 21/346 48 11, Category 1–2*

Tavares Rico (U/C–D 4)

18th century ambience, walls with ormolu mirrors. Value for money lunches on the first floor (canteen). *Rua da Misericórdia 37, Tel. 21/342 11 12, Category 1–2*

T-Clube (O)

You cannot spend a more pleasant evening anywhere else. Included are a bar, restaurant and discotheque under one roof. Stylish, with a view of the Discovery Monument. *Av. de Brasília, Tel. 21/301 66 52, Category 1–2*

CAFÉS

The city's best known café (the Bohemians once gathered here) is the *Brasileira* on the *Largo do Chiado.* The *Confeitaria Nacional* on the *Praça da Figueira* is a quiet oasis. The *Martinho da Arcada* café-restaurant on the *Praça Comércio* is the oldest in the city. Also rich in tradition is the *Suiça* on the *Rossio.* Definitely worth seeing are the Art Déco fittings and furnishings in the *Nicola (Rossio)* and the dainty decoration in the *Versailles (Av, da República).*

SHOPPING

Three main shopping districts: the most expensive lies in the region of the *Avenida s Novas*, around the

Avenida da Roma (**O**). The cheapest and busiest is within the old city walls, in the *Baixa* (**U/D 4–5**) with its streets all meeting at right angles. The street names reflect the guilds which once predominated here: *Rua da Prata* (silver) or *Rua dos Sapateiros* (shoemakers). In the *Chiado* district (around *Rua Garrett)* the shops are smarter but also more expensive than those in the Baixa. In Greater Lisbon there are four large shopping complexes: *Amoreiras* in the *Rua Duarte Pacheco* (**U/A 1–2**), *CascaiShopping* (**O**, *25 km outside the city on the N 9 near Alcabideche),* *Centro Vasco da Gama* (**O**), the latest shopping centre on the Expo site and the famous *CCC Centro Comercial Colombo* (**O**) opposite the Benfica Lisbon football stadium. This superlative shrine to consumerism is a must for all "shopaholics".

ACCOMMODATION

In the vicinity of the Rossio (in the *Rua das Portas de Santo Antao),* for example, there are many small guest houses charging reasonable rates.

Hotel da Lapa (**O**)
High-class city hotel. *99 rooms, Rua do Pau de Bandeira 4, Tel. 21/395 00 05, Fax 395 06 65, Category 1*

Hotel Lisboa Plaza (**U/C–D 3**)
In a quiet side street only two minutes from the city centre. Stylish, elegant. *112 rooms, Av. da Liberdade/Travessa Salitre, Tel. 21/346 39 22, Fax 347 16 30, Category 1*

Hotel Métropole (**U/D 4**)
A tastefully renovated hotel in the city centre. *36 rooms, Rossio 30, Tel. 21/346 91 64, Fax 346 91 66, Category 1–2*

Pensão Ninho das Águias (**U/E 4**)
Typical guest house at the foot of São Jorge Castle. *14 rooms, Costa do Castelo 74, Tel. 21/886 70 08, Category 3*

York House (**U/A 5**)
In a former 16th century convent, an elegant residence with much charm, a pretty inner courtyard and beautiful rooms. *32 rooms, Rua das Janelas Verdes 32, Tel. 21/396 24 35, Fax 397 27 93, Category 1*

ENTERTAINMENT

Night life starts late in Lisbon. There is no need to set out before 10.30 pm unless you are going to the *cinema* – in Portugal this is an experience which will take up the whole evening: the performance *(cost about $ 800)* usually starts after 8.30 pm and, with brief intervals, often lasts until 11 pm, after which the audience goes for a meal. *Fado bars* do open from about 8 pm but there is little going on until 10 pm. Most fado establishments lie in the Barro Alto, many require a *minimum charge ranging from $ 3000* per person. The locals happily recommend the non-touristy fado in *A Viela (Open Mon–Sat),* in the *Cristal* or the one in the *Casa do Leão* in the Castelo São Jorge in the Alfama district *(Open Tue, Thu, Fri).*

In Lisbon the Tejo (Tagus) district is becoming an ever more popular place to live and the same goes for its night life. Admittedly you will find a plethora of interesting bars and pubs *(Café Targus, Frágil, Trés Pastorinhos, Pavilhão*

Chinês, Páginas Tantas) but there is even more going on in the industrial area and in the docks down by the Tejo: Alcântara is the name of the quarter which has blossomed into the "in" place to meet. There you will find bars and pubs by the *Santo Amaro Docks*, discos in the warehouses near *Rua da Cintura do Porto de Lisboa (Kings and Queens, Indochina* and *Blues Café)* and a rendezvous on *Avenida 24 de Julho*. Popular too is the somewhat freaky *Trifásica* café-bar near Lisbon's finest discotheque, the *Kapital*. The discos known as *Alcântara Mar* (in the centre of the industrial area), *Salsa Latina* (in a warehouse by the river), *Stones, Kapital, Kremlin* and *Plateau* (all on *Av. 24 de Julho)* do not fill up until the early hours of the morning. The more mature prefer to go to the *T-Clube* in *Belém* close by the Discovery Monument.

INFORMATION

Turismo **(U/D 4)**
Praça dos Restauradores, Tel. 21/346 63 07, Fax 346 87 72, and also at the *airport*

SURROUNDING AREA

Cascais **(112/A 2)**
A tourist centre on a small bay. Many cafés and boutiques. Hopelessly crowded in summer. There are *azulejos* to be seen in the old *Town Hall* and in the chapel of *Nossa Senhora da Nazare*. The largest shopping centre in Greater Lisbon; *CascaiShopping*

Estoril **(112/A–B 2)**
Was at one time "the" seaside resort of Portugal. Good hotels *(e.g. Hotel Palácio, 168 rooms, Rua do Parque, Tel. 21/468 04 00, Fax 468 48 67, Category 1),* casino, golf courses. There are many 17th and 18th century country estates in the region; some are open to visitors, e.g. the *palace* of the Counts of Pombal in *Oeiras*.

Palmela **(112/C 3)**
Known for its good wine and the colourful wine festival in September. In an old castle with a museum (local history and temporary exhibitions) on a hill just outside the town in the Setúbal direction lies the beautiful *Pousada de Palmela (28 rooms, Tel. 21/235 12 26, Fax 233 04 40, Category 1).*

SINTRA

(112/A 2) ★ At the foot of a thickly wooded rocky mountain which has been designated a World Cultural Heritage Site by UNESCO, lies Sintra (Pop. c.20,000), once the summer residence of Portuguese kings and noblemen. Narrow little streets with picturesque nooks and crannies, rococo villas, hidden chalets and the mild climate all combine to attract many visitors.

SIGHTS

Palácio Nacional da Pena
In the centre of a subtropical park on a rocky crag high above Sintra stands the Palácio da Pena built in the mid 19th century. It is a strange fantasy building in a mix of various styles. *Open Tue–Sun 10 am–5 pm, admission $ 400, free on Sun mornings.*

Palácio da Vila (Royal Palace)
The Manueline palace is a labyrinthian complex from the

15th/16th centuries with inner courtyards in the Moorish style, impressive *azulejos* and extravagant interior furnishings. Its huge chimneys have become a town symbol. *Open daily 10 am–1 pm and 2–5 pm, admission $ 400, free on Sun mornings.*

MUSEUM

Museu de Arte Moderna
The museum houses the Berardo Collection with some major works by European and American artists of the post-war period. *Open Wed–Sun 10 am–6 pm, Tue 2–6 pm, admission $ 600, Av. Heliodoro Salgado*

RESTAURANT

Adraga
A simple fish restaurant on the secluded beach with a view of the surf. *Praia da Adraga, Tel. 21/929 08 72, Category 3*

ACCOMMODATION

Caesar Park
A luxury hotel in a nature reserve 6 km outside the town. 18-hole golf course. *177 rooms, Linhó, tel. 21/924 90 11, Fax 924 90 07, Category 1*

Lawrence's Hotel
This is how the dukes must once have lived. *22 rooms, Rua Consiglieri Pedroso 38–40, Tel. 21/910 55 00, Fax 910 55 05, Category 1–2*

Pensão Sintra
Everything is superb right down to the furnishings: the former mansion, the garden, the pool, the tranquillity. *10 rooms, Travessa dos Avelares 12, Tel. 21/923 07 38, Category 2*

INFORMATION

Turismo
Praça da República, Tel. 21/923 11 57, Fax 923 51 76

SURROUNDING AREA

Cabo da Roca   (112/A 2)
★ The westernmost point of the European mainland. A lighthouse stands on the cliffs which are at least 140 m high and buffeted by the wind.

Guincho   (112/A 1)
The world surfing championships are held annually on Guincho beach. The fort on the cliffs is now an hotel (worth seeing!) *(Hotel do Guincho, 31 rooms, Tel. 21/487 04 91, Fax 487 04 31, Category 1)*

Mafra   (112/B 1)
This massive palace was commissioned by King João V in the early 18th century. Its most interesting feature is the huge *library* with bookshelves 88 metres long. *Open Wed–Mon 10 am–1 pm and 2–5 pm, admission $ 350, free on Sun mornings*

Peniche and Ericeira   (108/A 3–5)
The region's best surfing spots – for professionals only! Information from the *Ericeira Surf Clube (Rua Eduardo Burnay, Tel./Fax 261/86 63 99)*

Queluz   (112/B 2)
A serene little rococo palace with pretty gardens, small woods and a waterfall. The palace building is today a hotel with a restaurant, the *Cozinha Velha,* stylish but expensive *(Tel. 21/435 61 58, Category 1).*

In the wide Alentejo

*A lonely expanse, shimmering in the heat,
which deserves more attention than it usually receives*

The "Plains" is the name given to this large, wide and flat region which extends south-east on each side of the Tejo (Tagus). At one time these provinces were called Ribatejo and Alentejo, namely, the countryside on the banks *(riba)* and on the far side *(além)* of the Tejo. In summer it is unbearably hot there, in autumn it rains cats and dogs, the winters are bitterly cold and there is barely any spring. The land is thinly populated and is the poorest area in Portugal. Most tourists drive through it without paying much attention, because for miles there is very little to see: a monotonous landscape. just a hill here and there. Between the widely separated villages you will repeatedly come across a *monte*, a white estate house on a hill. These are the estates which were appropriated by the impoverished but proud farm workers after the 1974 revolution and subsequently operated as co-operatives. Gradually, however, these land reforms were reversed by the government. Around such

The Roman Temple in Évora, once bricked up, was not uncovered until the 19th century

montes fields of corn, meadows and cork oak forests stretch as far as the eye can see. Quite often you will come across large herds of pigs, sheep and cattle and it comes as no surprise to learn that more than a third of all Portuguese livestock is reared on these giant estates. The region is by no means as boring, quiet and melancholy, barren and endless as it might appear as you drive through it. There are green meadows, olive groves and cork oaks. In the plains, too, there are places of interest and many opportunities for the visitor.

BEJA

(114/A 5) Because of its location Beja is also known as the Queen of the Plains: coming from the north you will recognise the town, commandingly situated on a hill, from afar by its castle and the massive tower; the new buildings on the edge of town tend to hide the fact that in the centre lies a charming Old Town with narrow little streets and an attractive pedestrian zone. Beja (Pop. c.36,000) is a pretty little place in which to wander around; at every step the visitor will find remains of the town's eventful past, redolent of the Romans, Visigoths and Moors who once lived here. A few hours should suffice to see all the attractions of this, the second largest town in the Alentejo, but it would repay a more leisurely visit.

SIGHTS

Praça da República

Here stand the *pelourinho* (Manueline stocks), the old and the new *town halls* and the *Church of the Misericórdia* (in strict Renaissance style); it was originally designed to be an abattoir and was not converted to a church until the 16th century.

Torre de Menagem

◁▷ The town symbol and part of the massive castle which was built on Roman foundations and at one time had 40 gates; only a few still survive. It is well worth while climbing up the 40 m high 13th century tower, the tallest defensive tower in the whole country. *Open Tue–Sun 10 am–1 pm and 2–6 pm, in winter until 4 pm only, admission $ 150, free on Sun*

MUSEUM

Museu da Rainha Dona Leonor

The local museum is housed in the former Conceição Convent (Manueline style). This convent has become famous because of the love letters from the nun Mariana to the Count of Chamilly. Today it is rumoured that the love letters were in fact not written by the love-sick nun but by a Frenchman. In the church are some old Moorish *azulejos* and in the museum you

can see local history and sacred exhibits. *Open Tue–Sun 9.45 am–1 pm and 2–5.15 pm, admission $ 200*

RESTAURANTS/CAFÉ

Café Luis da Rocha

❖ The town's best known café. While it is not cosy or particularly cheap it is typical of Portuguese small town cafés and usually full; a speciality of the house is *porquinhos* – little chocolate piglets. There is a restaurant on the first floor. *Rua Capitão João Francisco de Sousa*

Esquina

❖ At present the most popular restaurant among the locals. *Rua Infante Dom Henrique 24, Tel. 284/38 92 38, Category 3*

Os Infantes

❖ Bar and restaurant with good cuisine which is located at the southern exit from the town. *Rua dos Infantes 14, Tel. 284/227 89, Category 2*

O Portão

A simple, cheap establishment. *Travessa da Audiência, Tel. 284/233 12, Category 3*

SHOPPING

On the first and third Mondays in each month there is a large market on the *Largo da Feira* (at the exit from the town going towards the Algarve). Annual markets and folk festivals are held in the second half of May and from 10 to 15 August. On 10 August, St Lourenço's (St Lawrence's) Day, there is a colourful folk festival, together with bull fights.

MARCO POLO SELECTION: PLANÍCIES

1 Portalegre
This old episcopal seat is worth a visit because of its beautiful urban features which include palaces, churches, convents, burghers' houses and a town wall (page 75)

2 Almendres
Prehistoric finds, megalithic tombs and stone circles make a tour worthwhile (page 75)

3 The Roman Temple of Évora
One of the best-preserved Roman ruins in Portugal (page 74)

4 Casa dos Ossas in Évora
Anyone who has visited the little chapel will never forget it; a whole room is clad with the bones of more than 5,000 people (page 74)

ACCOMMODATION

Most guest houses are right in the town centre.

Residencial Bejense
Cheap, simple and centrally situated. *24 rooms, Rua Capitao João Francisco de Sousa 57, Tel. 284/32 50 01/02, Category 3*

Hotel Residencial Melius
Comfortable and modern hotel. *62 rooms, Rua Fialho de Almeida, Tel. 284/32 18 22, Fax 32 18 25, Category 2*

Pousada de São Francisco
Established as recently as 1994 in the old 13th century Franciscan convent, it is one of the most beautiful pousadas in Portugal. *35 rooms, Tel. 284/32 84 41, Fax 32 91 43, Category 1*

ENTERTAINMENT

In the evenings people patronise *Ufo's* bar or the *Via Ferrea* and *República do Alcool* discotheques.

Café-Bar Os Infantes
A favourite rendezvous of intellectuals; there is often live music as well as art exhibitions. *From 10 pm, Rua dos Infantes 14*

INFORMATION

Turismo
Praça da República, Tel. 284/31 01 50, Fax 31 01 51

SURROUNDING AREA

Moura (114/C 4)
It is clear to the onlooker that this little spa town (Pop. 10,000), some 60 km north-east of Beja, is Moorish in character, as is also indicated by its name which means "the Moorish (town)". It lies white as snow against the surrounding landscape. On the main square is the entrance to the little spa gardens with a ৶৶ viewing terrace.

ÉVORA

(114/A 2-3) Some three hundred men are standing around in groups chatting. They are discussing social injustices, politics and the price of livestock – above all they are doing business together. The ❂ Praça do Geraldo, the arcaded town square of Évora, the capital of the Alentejo, is the meeting place on Tuesday mornings of dealers and farmers from all around: a market without goods. You can forget about driving the car along here.

The historic town centre with its 16th and 17th century burghers' houses, the old palaces and churches in various architectural styles and the narrow little one-way streets with their nooks and crannies is surrounded by medieval walls dating from the 14th century. It still has a somewhat Moorish appearance and is sometimes called "cidade museu" – museum city.

The town (Pop. c.52,000) is rich in monuments, which is why UNESCO has placed the whole under a preservation order and on the list of Cultural Heritage Sites.

SIGHTS

Casa dos Ossos
★ A macabre attraction is the 17th century Chapel of Bones in the church of São Francisco. The walls of the chapel are covered with 5,000 skulls and bones. This is not recommended for visitors of a sensitive disposition. A small plaque warns visitors: *Nós ossos que aqui estamos – pelos vossos esperamente*: "Our bones assembled here are awaiting yours". *Open*

daily 9 am–1 pm and 2–5.30 pm, until 6 pm in summer, admission $ 50

Sé (Cathedral)
The 12th/13th church with its 70 m long nave and Europe's oldest organ is impressive. The building was started in 1186 and is a severe fortress-like structure. Unfortunately the tower is unsafe and can no longer be climbed. Of interest are the *convent* adjoining the cathedral with its medieval cloister and the *Museu de Arte Sacra*; the major items in its collection are a reliquary crucifix with 146 precious stones and diamonds, and an ebony Madonna (13th/14th century). The triptych shows ten scenes from the life of Mary. *Open Tue–Sun 10 am–midday and 2–5 pm, admission $ 250*

Templo Romano
★ Only 14 of the original 18 Corinthian columns of this temple (1st/2nd century) are still standing; it was bricked up for hundreds of years and thus safeguarded from collapse. The bricks were not removed until 1870. The temple is said to have been dedicated to the Goddess Diana, but nobody has yet been able to prove this.

RESTAURANTS

Aquário
❂ Very popular with the locals and therefore well patronised. *Rua de Valdevinos 7, Tel. 266/294 03, Category 2*

Fialho
A veritable gastronomic temple, the best restaurant in the whole region. *Travessa das Mascarenhos 16, Tel. 266/230 79, Category 1–2*

Al Gharb means "The West"

The Moors gave this name to the western part of their emirate, and the Spaniards retained it after the reconquista

The country's most southerly province, the Algarve, was the last to come under the rule of the Portuguese crown 700 years ago. This coastal strip, 50 km wide and 150 km long, on the southern Atlantic coast of Portugal, is separated from Spain to the east by the Rio Guadiana and from the Alentejo in the north by a range of mountains. The latter protects the region from the cold north winds and makes it rather like a rich garden. Here grow olive and carob trees, oranges, lemons, figs and almonds. In January and February the famous almond blossom turns the region into a rose-pink paradise.

The coastal landscape is also extremely varied: in the east there are extensive sandbanks, dunes and lagoons, in the west ever more rocky coasts and steep cliffs. The combination of a mild climate, old cultures and beautiful beaches has for more than a hundred years made the Algarve a popular place for a

Sandy bays can also be found in the rocky western part of the Algarve

holiday. Unfortunately mass tourism has ruined large tracts of the countryside: modern hotel complexes and giant holiday settlements are destroying the coastal scene.

However, new regional environmental plans should help and a real attempt is being made to preserve the romantic little fishing villages and quiet beaches as the travel agents promise us they will. So, for example, if you stand in the nature reserve near Sagres where "the land ends and the sea begins", or on the windy cliffs of the Cabo de São Vicente and look out to sea, perhaps you will sense how beautiful it must once have been here.

The Marco Polo Guide to the Algarve provides more detailed information.

ALBUFEIRA

(116/C 5) Albufeira is the tourist centre *par excellence*. At the same time it must be said that there is very little to see in the old fishing town (Pop. 21,000) ; the museum is closed, the famous caves have collapsed and the viewing platform has been built over. Nevertheless Albufeira has a certain charm and a beautiful location. The little square in the old town centre and the adjoining pedestrian zone are bustling with activity; the many small cafés, restaurants and bars are bursting at the seams in summer and offer just what young people on holiday want. Admittedly Albufeira has not escaped the building boom but the town planners have managed to ensure that the new blends with the old. Laid out in terraces, the whitewashed houses sparkle against the blue sea.

RESTAURANTS

There are many pretty restaurants in Albufeira; recommended: *A Ruína, Tel. 289/51 20 94, Category 2* (rustic), ✪ *As Três Palmeiras* (outside the town in *Areias de São João*, popular with the locals), *Tel. 289/58 63 53, Category 2.*

SHOPPING

A ✪ large *market* is held in the Orada district of town on the first and third Tuesday of every month.

ACCOMMODATION

Club Aldiana Algarve
This bungalow complex was opened in 1998 and lies on the steep coast between Albufeira and Vilamoura with an extensive beach. It has a golf course and tennis courts, an outdoor and an indoor pool. *285 rooms, Rocha Baixinha, Tel. 289/54 01 00, Fax 54 01 99, Category 1*

Rocamar
Hotel above the sea with a

MARCO POLO SELECTION: ALGARVE

1 Trip to Alcoutim by steamboat
A trip from Vila Real to Alcoutim through charming countryside along the River Guadiana which forms part of the border (page 82)

2 Faro hinterland
The short journey from Santa Bárbara to Estói is worthwhile for the beautiful scenery (page 82)

3 Almansil
In the village church visitors can admire the *azulejos* by the Baroque painter Policarpo (pages 81–82)

4 Burgau
This little fishing "nest" appears to be almost glued into a wide cleft in the rocks; there is no space for a proper harbour, the fishing boats are simply lifted up to the village street (page 85)

5 Vila do Bispo
17th century parish church with some superb *azulejos* (page 86)

6 Cabo de São Vicente
The most south-westerly cape in Europe is something for nature lovers (page 86)

The little old fishing port of Albufeira has become a tourist centre par excellence – with all the advantages and disadvantages

superb view over the bay. The beach is accessible by means of steps. *91 rooms, Largo Jacinto d'Ayet, Tel. 289/58 69 90, Fax 58 69 98, Category 3*

Vila Vita Parc

The most beautiful holiday complex in the Algarve is at Armaçao de Pêra; it offers excellent standards of comfort and service and a unique park. *158 rooms, Armaçao de Péra, Tel. 282/31 53 10, Fax 31 53 33, Category 1*

SPORTS & LEISURE

Golf: golf enthusiasts are spoilt for choice: there are 19 courses in the Algarve. The most famous one in the country is the *Royal Golf Course*. The *Pine Cliffs* boasts a magnificent panoramic view. The *Penina* course is a masterpiece designed by Sir Henry Cotton. The best short course for practice is the *Vale de Milho*. Those seeking to test their skills to the utmost should try the *Salgados* course.

Sailing and boat excursions: in nearby *Vilamoura* various firms (e.g. *Algarve Seafaris* or *Cascais Marina Tour*) offer short sailing trips – also powerboats and fishing trips. *Day tour including barbecue from $ 6,150*

✝ Bathing: Outside Albufeira (buses from all outlying places) lie the amusement parks known as *The Big One, Slide & Splash* and *Atlântica. Admission $ 2,400, children $ 1,500.*

The *Zoomarine Park* with dolphin shows will interest the children. *Admission $ 2,450, children $ 1,500*

Jeep safaris into the interior can be booked through *Zebra Safari, Tel. 289/58 87 96*

❂ *Bull fights* are held on *Saturday afternoons* during the summer months. *Admission from $ 4,000*

ENTERTAINMENT

Albufeira, especially the Rua dos Bares, is the centre of Algarve night life. Unsurpassed: *Central Station*, a combined café, bar, disco and ice cream parlour on two floors. You simply must see *Kadoc* (the best disco in Portugal), *IRS* (interesting decor) and *El Divino* (bands are flown in from Cuba). Completely new is the *Wa-Wa-Club* in *Vilamoura*, an exclusive dance hall for the more mature clientele.

INFORMATION

Turismo
Rua 5 de Outubro, Tel. 289/58 52 79

FARO

(117/D–E 6) Admittedly Faro does not have a very beautiful town silhouette and is often thought of as an uninspiring industrial and administrative centre (Pop. c.51,000), but it is in fact a town with charm and much greenery (palm trees). A long lagoon and a pretty town centre are well worth a visit. The old quarter is still surrounded by medieval fortified walls with massive towers. The Moors ruled here for more than five hundred years until King Afonso III liberated his country from them in 1249. The disastrous earthquake of 1755 destroyed many of the fine buildings.

SIGHTS

Old Town
At the end of the ❂ *Jardim Manuel Bivar* park by the harbour is the entrance to the Old Town: the *Arco da Vila*. In a niche in the Renaissance gateway stands a statue of Faro's patron saint, St Thomas Aquinas. To the left near the town gate is the tourist office. The Old Town is known as *Vila a dentro*; it is surrounded by massive fortified walls. On its beautiful main square *Largo da Sé* – orange trees grow here – stands the 13th century *cathedral (Open Mon–Fri 10 am–midday, Sun after mass)*. Apart from the solid entrance tower it was destroyed in the 1755 earthquake. Today it reflects a mixture of Gothic, Renaissance and baroque styles. Interior: 17th century rosary chapel with *azulejos*.

MUSEUMS

Museu Arqueológico e Lapidar Infante Dom Henrique
A former Capuchin convent: paintings, *azulejos*, early historical finds and Roman mosaics. *Open Mon–Fri 10 am–midday and 2–5 pm, admission $ 250, Praça Afonso III (behind the cathedral)*

Museu Etnográfico

Interesting portrayal of the life and work of the people of the region. *Open Tue–Sat 10 am–6 pm, admission $ 300, Rua Pé da Cruz 2*

Museu Marítimo Ramalho Ortigão

The maritime museum provides an insight into method of fishing, displaying models of boats, fishing gear, pictures of voyages, marine maps and a collection of fish and crustaceans. *Open Mon–Fri 10 am–midday and 2–5 pm, admission $ 200, north-western corner of the boat harbour.*

RESTAURANTS

In Faro there are plenty of cafés and restaurants to relax in. Typical street cafés can be found by the municipal gardens and in the adjoining pedestrian zone, the ✪ *Rua de Santo António.* Pubs and bars are in *Rua Filipe Alistão, Rua Conselheiro Bivar* and on the square known as *Ferreira de Almeida,* for example, the garden pub *Sol e Jardím* (mainly students) or the cheap ✪ *Centenário* in *Rua Lethes*; both *Category 3*. The locals consider the best restaurant in town to be the *O Gargalo (Largo do Pé da Cruz 30, Tel. 289/273 05, Category 1)*. The jetset meets in the *Restaurante Camané (Praia de Faro, Tel. 289/81 75 39, Category 1.* ⤵ *La Réserve* in *Santa Bárbara de Nexe* is very stylish (excellent cuisine). There you can sit on the terrace and enjoy the magnificent view of the villages around Faro *(prior booking essential, Tel. 289/99 92 34, Category 1).*

SHOPPING

Faro's favourite shopping street is Rua de Santo António with its many small side streets. There is a ✪ *daily market from 6 am–1 pm* on the square known as *Dr Francisco de Sá Carneiro. Pecas Soltas (Praça D. Francisco Gomes)* stocks fashion clothes by top Portuguese designers.

ACCOMMODATION

Hotel Eva

Right by the harbour, a modern hotel. *135 rooms, Av. da República 1, Tel. 289/80 33 54, Fax 80 23 04, Category 1*

SPORTS & LEISURE

Praia de Faro, Faro's beach, lies 8 km to the south of the town on a long stretch of sandbank; sailing boats and fishing gear can be hired here. There is also a windsurfing school. There are golf courses in the *Vale do Lobo* and at the *Quinta do Lago Golf Club.* Both lie about 15 km west of Faro.

ENTERTAINMENT

The hustle and bustle of Faro's night life centres on *Concelheiro do Bivar* and *Rua do Prior.* There can be found lively bars, pubs and discos to meet the taste of every customer.

INFORMATION

Turismo

Rua da Misericórdia 8–12, Tel. 289/80 36 04

SURROUNDING AREA

Almansil   (117/D 5)

This tiny village on the N 125

coast road to the west is famous for the nearby ★ church of São Lourenço dos Matos. About 270 years ago the original Romanesque church was clad with azulejos by the Baroque painter Policarpo de Oliveira Bernardes.

Inland from Faro (117/D–E 5)

★ A delightful afternoon excursion takes you to Estói (11 km north of Faro). The place is known for its little late 18th century palace and especially for the wild and overgrown palace garden. This was modelled on Italian baroque gardens and is adorned with some superb azulejos, statues, rococo fountains

Modelled on Italian baroque gardens: the palace garden of Estói

and groups of figures. About 1 km away lie the Milreu Ruins (Open Tue–Sun 10 am–midday and 2–5 pm, admission free), which are the excavated remains of the Roman town of Ossonoba. Further west through some austere and rather dry countryside lies ✪ Santa Bárbara de Nexe, a tiny and very pretty place in the hills north of Faro; on Sundays the men stand at the crossroads and engage in serious discussion. A brief look in the church is very worthwhile in order to see the beautiful azulejos and the ormolu wood carvings.

Tavira (117/E–F 5)

This little fishing town lies on both sides of the mouth of the Rio Gilão: an original Roman bridge links the two equally charming sections of the town. Tavira is dominated by an old castle from where there is a fine view of the town. It is a pretty little town in which to stroll and have a coffee. In Tavira you can bathe only from an offshore sandbank, as is the case everywhere in this part of the Algarve.

Vila Real de Santo António (117/F 5)

This small town has not yet been spoiled by the building boom and has a Spanish feel; there is a youth hostel and a romantic grand hotel. From here you can take a ★ steamboat trip of some 30 km to Alcoutim on the Guadiana river (which here forms the border with Spain), passing through some lovely countryside. Reservation recommended

LAGOS

(116/B 5) A friendly little town standing on a heavily built-up hill, with an Old Town of white-washed houses, many narrow and twisting little streets (not suitable for cars), an attractive pedestrian zone and a number of small squares, ideal for a relaxing stroll. Tourists are attracted by the many bathing bays, the nearby marine caves, the magnificent ◁▷ rock formations and the chance to walk in the footsteps of Henry the Navigator. It was in the 15th century that the great explorer set out from this former Roman settlement. His shipyards built the caravelles for the voyages of discovery. 500 years ago Europe's first slave market was held here. For nearly two hundred years – until 1756 – Lagos was the capital of the Algarve; today this pretty little town (Pop. at least 16,000) is an important fishing and shipbuilding centre.

SIGHTS

The best view of the massive 14th–16th century town walls which surround much of the Old Town can be had from the landing stage near the castle on the fishing harbour.

Doreal marzipan factory
The marzipan tradition in the Algarve stems from the Moors who grew almond trees in a big way. A visit to this factory is a must for all those with a sweet tooth. *Open Mon–Fri 9.30 am–5.30 pm, on the extension to the river bank promenade, going in the Sagres direction*

Praça da República
The focal point of the town with a *statue* of Henry the Navigator (1960), the scene of the former slave market (in the old customs house under the arcades), the *governor's palace* and the *Church of the Misericórdia*.

Church of Santo António
The 18th century baroque chapel is known as the "Golden Chapel" because of the many gilded wood carvings and the superb *azulejos*; it is a part of the adjoining municipal museum and really worth a visit.

MUSEUM

Museu Municipal de Lagos
As well as archaeological finds and some documents relating to the town's history, the municipal museum – which is linked to the church of Santo Antonio – has an impressive collection of folk art portraying the rural life and work of the fisherfolk (also very interesting to children). *Open Tue–Fri 9.30 am–midday and 2–5 pm, admission $ 340, Rua General Alberto da Silveira*

RESTAURANTS

There are many restaurants in the Rua 25 de Abril pedestrian zone in the town centre. In summer a three-day ✿ festival of regional sweetmeats is held on the Mercado do Levante.

Dom Sebastião
Stylishly rustic with good cuisine. *Rua 25 de Abril 20–22, Tel. 282/76 27 95, Category 2*

O Galeão
Courteous service by candlelight. *Rua da Laranjeira 1, Tel. 282/76 39 09, Category 2*

Unprepossessing from the outside: the "Golden Chapel" of Santo António in Lagos

Quinta dos Areões

An old estate about 6 km in the Sagres direction, just beyond Espiche; folk-festival atmosphere with good plain food, singing and dancing, folk music on Wednesdays. *Self-service from $ 5,500 per person including drinks, Tel. 282/78 94 51*

Restaurante Reis

❂ Many local people regularly can be found here. *Rua António Barbosa Vianna 21, Tel. 282/76 29 00, Category 2–3*

Vai e Volta

An earthy *tasca* to satisfy large appetites at a small price. *Rua Infante do Sagres, Tel. 282/76 88 06, Category 3*

SHOPPING

In the mornings there is a ❂ fish market near the *Praça Gil Eanes*. On the first Saturday in each month there is a *tourist market* at the Portimão exit from the town.

ACCOMMODATION

Hotel Bela Vista da Luz

A new hotel situated 6 km to the west in Praia da Luz. *164 rooms, Tel. 282/78 86 55, Fax 78 86 56, Category 1–2*

Hotel De Lagos

A modern establishment in the Moorish style near the town centre. Shuttle service to the beach. *304 rooms, Rua Nova da Aldeia, Tel. 282/76 99 67, Fax 76 99 20, Category 1*

Albergaria Marina Rio

36 rooms. Try to get one with a sea view! Sun terrace and pool. *Av. dos*

*Descombrimentos 388, Tel. 282/76
98 59, Fax 76 99 60, Category 2*

SPORTS & LEISURE

In the immediate vicinity of
Lagos there are 15 magnificent
beaches surrounded by massive
rock formations; the smallest
beach *(Praia dos Estudantes)* is only
50 metres long (it is the second
one going towards Sagres).

❀ *Bull fights*, so popular with
the Portuguese, are held on Saturday afternoons *from May to
October. Admission $ 4,000*

Golf at the *Palmares Golf Club* (3
km to the east) and at the *Penina
Golf Club* (half way to Portimão).
Guides to walks in the region are
obtainable from the tourist office.

↘↗ A boat excursion along the
coast will be found rewarding; a
six-hour trip with lunch on the
beach costs from $ 6,150. *Orga-
nizer: Via Sagres, Tel. 282/76 76 41*
(can also be booked from other
towns at an additional charge).

ENTERTAINMENT

The *Bon Vivant* bar is a popular
meeting place, young people
prefer the ⚲*Phoenix* discotheque,
and those with a penchant for loud
music should visit ⚲*Mullens* bar.
The largest disco-bar in Lagos is the
XL Casino in *Alvor* (near Portimão).

INFORMATION

Turismo
*Largo Marquês de Pombal, Tel.
282/76 30 31*

SURROUNDING AREA

Alvor   (116/B 5)
This tiny resort between Por-
timão and Lagos lies at the estuary of the Rio Alvor. Well worth
seeing is the Manueline doorway
of the little *village church*. The
Caleidoscópio shop sells handbags,
jewellery, ties and waistcoats
made from natural cork.

Burgau   (116/B 6)
★ Everything in Burgau is small:
the beach, the streets and the
pubs. So that you do not unex-
pectedly drive into the sea – the
steep village street simply ends
on the beach – it is best to park
in the vicinity of the tiny square
(more like a largish street junc-
tion). Some older visitors like to
rent properties here for the
winter months.

Ponta da Piedade   (116/B 5–6)
↘↗ You can in fact drive to the
Ponta da Piedade, but it is much
nicer to take a boat trip along the
steep rugged coast to the cape
with its droll rock formations
which are the most beautiful
anywhere along the Algarve
coast. In the season from May to
October local fishermen ferry
visitors to the marine caves.
*Departure from Lagos quay, cost per
boat from $ 4,000*

Portimão   (116/B 5)
A busy port (Pop. c.45,000) with-
out much charm. Only in August,
during the "Festival da Sardinhas",
can you get some idea of what it
must have been like at one time.

Praia da Rocha   (116/B 5)
As early as the beginning of the
twentieth century Praia da
Rocha, with its long beaches of
soft sand and superb rock formations, began to attract tourists.
Today the resort is littered with

high-rise buildings and apartment blocks. However, the tasteful *Bela Vista urban villa* warrants a look: it is now a bed and breakfast hotel *(14 rooms, Av. Tomás Cabreira, Tel. 282/45 04 80, Fax 41 53 69, Category 1)*. The 19th century staircase with its *azulejos* is interesting, and a drink on the terrace with its view of the wide beach is worthwhile.

Sagres (116/A 6)

The journey there is more interesting than the town itself (Pop. 4,000). More attractive than the main road is the stretch via Luz, Burgau and Salema (although that from Burgau to Salema is only a dirt track). Sagres lies in raw and austere countryside near to ★ *Cabo de São Vicente*, the most south-westerly point in Europe (you can visit the ⚬ lighthouse but it is not always open).

The nearby *fortaleza* is where Henry is said to have established his school of navigation. You can search in vain for any remains, however. Moreover, recently new exhibition halls have been built over the ruins of former commercial buildings. Anglers fish from the cliffs in any weather. The massive *wind-rose*, which probably dates from the 15th century, and stands at the entrance to the castle is said to have magic powers in the moonlight. There is a *market* in Sagres on the first Friday in the month.

Serra de Monchique (116/B 4–5)

⚬ Only in good weather should you undertake the winding journey 30 km inland to the old spa town of Caldas de Monchique with its *fin de siècle* ambience and its warm springs. There is the opportunity for some good walks here. The mimosa and camellia blossom is magnificent in winter. You can stop off at the *Bica Boa restaurant, (Tel. 282/91 22 71, Category 2)* and relax on the sun-terrace. From Monchique an old ⚬ Way of the Cross leads up to the ruined *convent of Nossa Senhora de Desterro* from where there are wonderful views. There are *guided walks* and *moonlight walks* from mid-July to mid-September *(Tel. 282/91 10 41, adults $ 4,000, children $ 2,500)*.

Vila do Bispo (116/A 5–6)

★ The Baroque parish church of this little town with its interesting *azulejos* and ormolu wood carvings dates from the 17th century. Vila do Bispo has several times been praised for its water quality and clean beaches.

Para embrulhar

The Portuguese word for "to wrap up" is *embrulhar* – and the Portuguese just love wrapping things up! *Embrulhar* is almost a cult activity, it arouses anticipation, prolongs the enjoyment and increases the value of the wares.. The Portuguese fold boxes in an elaborate fashion and tie ribbons round them in a most artistic way. The actual packing itself is performed with relish like an act from a play, even in bakeries where *bolos* and *pasteis* are lovingly wrapped so that these tempting pastries with such suggestive names as "little breasts" or "nuns' tummies" will arrive home safely.

Nature in plenty and a lovers' wood

These routes are marked in green on the map on the inside front cover and in the Road Atlas beginning on page 100

① THREE DAYS THROUGH GREEN PORTUGAL

This round trip of some 500 km starts from Oporto and initially leads northwards along the coast as far as the Spanish border. The next day centres on the unspoilt Peneda Gerês National Park, while the third day is devoted mainly to the port wine region along the Douro. To allow sufficient time for sightseeing, a swim in the sea or in artificial lakes and for walks, you should plan to take at least three days.

The beauty and magic of the "green coast" will captivate you a soon as you leave Oporto and proceed north along the IC 1 expressway. The little provincial town of *Vila do Conde* should be your first stop (Wednesday is market day), for there you can visit the parish church, which has a beautiful rose window, and the former convent of Santa Clara – or have a cool swim on the fine sandy beach. From Vila do Conde a 7 km-long aqueduct (999 arches) stretches as far as *Póvoa de Varzim*, a neighbouring little fishing village and the birthplace of Eça de Queirós

(1845–1900), the most famous Portuguese novel writer of the 19th century. There is a monument to him outside the town hall. Wide stretches of the aqueduct are still preserved and are easily visible from the road.

Having returned to the main road and continued north, shortly beyond Apúlia and *Ofir* (page 35) with its beautiful beach, cross the Cávado River on a narrow bridge just before reaching its mouth and you will come to *Esposende*, a beautiful seaside resort (wide beach). The journey from Esposende to Viana will give you a brief foretaste of what to expect further north: blossoming gardens, fields of cabbages, potatoes and maize with *espigueiros*, the typical granite storehouses, vine arbours, green hills rich in woodland, while to your left from time to time you will glimpse the sparkling sea. *Viana do Castelo (page 39)* lies at the foot of Monte Santa Luzia (above you will find a Celtic settlement, a pilgrimage church, a luxury hotel and a marvellous view) and is certainly worth a visit. At least you should make time for a stroll to the market place (Friday is market day) and along the promenade by the river.

Beyond Viana do Castelo, which has a delightful setting at the mouth of the Rio Lima, the road runs very close to the sea as far as *Caminha*, a fishing village with the region's finest parish church. Here the road leaves the coast and continues inland along the wide estuary of the Minho river. Now the landscape becomes more and more beautiful: the river flows peacefully on its way, and on the opposite Spanish bank towers the majestic *Monte Santa Tecla* with over 100 round houses of an excavated Celtic settlement (crossing $ 500). The cemeteries with their chapel-like graves on the Portuguese side emphasise the peaceful picture created by the valley. On no account fail to enjoy the panoramic view from the fortress in *Valença do Minho* (*page 41*) down to the river and to Galicia beyond. This little border town is also a suitable place to spend the night.

On the next day take your leave of the Minho Valley and drive along the N 201 down to *Ponte de Lima* where you cross over the medieval bridge in this idyllic little town. Continue along the Lima river to *Ponte da Barca* (walk along the river bank), the starting-out point for an excursion into the *Peneda Gerês National Park* (*pages 35 and 41*). There are a number of approaches to this magnificent landscape of woods and mountains with deep gorges, large artificial lakes and rare fauna and flora. Our route chooses the entrance in Entre Ambos os Rios 13 km north-east of Ponte de Barca and leads upstream along the Lima river past the stone-built houses of Cidadelhe, via Lindoso and Spanish Lobios as far as the Portela do Homem Pass and then the Roman road by the artificial lake of Vilarinho das Furnas to Covide, São Bento (rest in the pousada) and *Braga* (*page 32*). Here, in the old seat of Portuguese kings and archbish-ops, is where you break your journey – even though from afar Braga may give the impression of being a modern industrial town. After experiencing nature in the national park you can now obtain a further insight into the country's history (Celtic settle-ment, cathedral) as well as seeing some artistic monuments (epis-copal palace, old mansions and burghers' houses). There are plenty of restaurants and hotels (*pages 33 and 34*).

Going from Braga to *Guimarães (page 35)* the next day should not take more than a half an hour. On no account simply drive straight through the "cradle of Portugal" because it was here that the Kingdom of Portugal was founded, and in any case a visit to the castle is worthwhile. The little wine town of *Amarante* on the N 101 on the bank of the Tâmega will again make you receptive to the beauties of nature. The N 101 continues along the heavily wooded and wildly romantic Serra do Marão to *Peso da Régua (page 49)*, the centre of the "Pais de Vinho", the Portuguese port wine region. From here it is worth making a detour: a one-hour train ride in old railcars takes you through a particularly beautiful vine-growing region to *Vila Real* (*page 45*). The ride there and back costs less than $ 850 and is well worth it.

Having returned to Régua, take the scenically beautiful but winding road to *Lamego* (*page 49*), a little provincial town which has retained all its old charm. The Way of the Cross up the mountain is the most photographed subject in this part of the country.

On the return journey to Oporto you stay on the left bank of the Douro and travel on the N 222 along the enchanting Barro river valley to *Resende* (Romanesque church) and to *Castelo de Paiva* (superb Quinta da Boa vista). In Entre-os-Rios you cross the Douro and take the N 108 back to Oporto.

② IN THE FOOTSTEPS OF PORTUGAL'S UNIQUE PAIR OF LOVERS

This day-long tour of some 240 km is made wholly against the background of Pedro and Inês, Portugal's tragic medieval lovers. As well as all kinds of romantic places where their prohibited assignations took place you will discover the major convents and castles of Central Portugal. The old university town of Coimbra is the setting-out point and also the point of return.

He was married, she was his wife's cousin. It was love at first sight – even before his wedding. But it was impossible for him to break off his engagement to Constance: a familiar case of duty first. His father would probably have disinherited him. Therefore the lovers had to meet in secret although after the death of Constance, Pedro brought Inês to court where they lived for four happy years. It was a passionate liaison, a love until death. For Inês was put to death, brutally murdered on the instructions of his father in their secret rendezvous in the little hunting forest near Coimbra, Portugal's best known university town.

The tale of Pedro and Inês is Portugal's, most touching love story – and it really did happen as described. Pedro, the king's son, revenged his sweetheart's death by fighting his father, Afonso IV, and ripping out the hearts of her murderers. When he himself became king a few years later he had the body of Inês exhumed, her face made up, dressed her in ceremonial robes and had her crowned as queen – a true case of love beyond the grave.

This all took place in the 14th century but thousands of young couples make the annual pilgrimage to *Coimbra* and to the *Quinta das Lágrimas (page 54)*, the little forest in which the lovers secretly met. Here at the "Spring of Tears", the very spot where the hideous crime was committed, today's couples swear eternal love. There can hardly be anything more romantic than a hot summer's night with a cool breeze rustling the bamboo leaves and the silhouettes of young lovers reflected in the water. The little wood with its exotic old trees and enchanted spring is open to all visitors even though the land is privately owned. In the middle of the grove stands an old mansion *(page 55)* in which many a king resided. Those with the necessary means can rent a room in the freshly renovated palace and read the story of the lovers in peace by the fireside in the small lounge.

From Coimbra the route passes through *Leiria (page 58)*, where King Dinis I, Pedro's grandfather, once resided in the royal palace high above the town, and then on to *Batalha* (page 57), to a Dominican abbey declared a World Cultural Heritage site by UNESCO. Pedro's illegitimate son had it built in gratitude for his victory over the Castilians in the battle (Portuguese *batalha*) of 1385. As King Joao I he founded the Avis dynasty and secured Portugal's independence. The massive convent building with its many towers, domes, columns, pillars and baldachins and decorated with beautiful Manueline ornaments is not only a magnificent example of Portuguese Late Gothic architecture but also a symbol of the Portuguese desire for liberty. Building started in 1388 and was not completed until 1533.

You will not fully appreciate how ardent and profound was the love of the prince for his Inês until you see the lovers' sarcophagi in the abbey of *Alcobaça (page 57)*, a sleepy little town about thirty minutes' drive from Batalha. Here the tombs of the sweethearts stand facing each other so that Pedro and Inês will look straight into each other's eyes on the Day of Judgement. UNESCO have also made this convent a Cultural Heritage site. The rules of the order prescribed that there must always be 999 monks present in the abbey. As well as prayer and meditation, until they were secularized in 1834 they also devoted themselves to providing education in public schools, to caring for the sick and, above all, to agriculture, so that the region became a model district for the growing of vines, fruit and vegetables.

Proceeding through *Fátima (page 59)*, a pilgrimage site with the tiny Chapel of the Manifestation on the vast square in front of the neo-classical basilica, our tour continues to *Tomar (page 58)*, the capital of the Knights Templar. It was here that Dinis I founded the Order of the Knights of Christ "to defend the faith, to fight the Moors and to exalt the Portuguese monarchy". With the help of the Castle of the Knights of Christ, one of the most beautiful monasteries in the country, the close links between the Order and the history of Portugal can be studied. Henry the Navigator, a grandson of Pedro and himself a Grand Master, was able to finance his voyages of discovery only with financial help from the Order.

On the way back to Coimbra (do not use the motorway, take the scenically more beautiful stretch via Pontao) you will pass by *Conimbriga (page 55)*, the "Portuguese Pompeii", Portugal's largest ruined Roman town with gateways, houses, halls and above all beautiful coloured mosaics.

Back in Coimbra you can again walk to the Santa Clara Convent, where Inês once lived, and look for the little stream on which Pedro sent his love letters to Inês.

Practical information

This section lists all the essential addresses and information you need for your visit to Portugal.

AMERICAN & BRITISH ENGLISH

Marco Polo travel guides are written in British English. In North America certain terms and usages deviate from British usage. Some of the more frequently encountered examples are (American given first): *baggage = luggage; cab = taxi; car rental = car hire; drugstore = chemist; fall = autumn; first floor = ground floor; freeway/highway = motorway; gas(oline) = petrol; railroad = railway; restroom = toilet/lavatory; streetcar = tram; subway = underground/tube; toll-free numbers = freephone numbers; trailer = caravan; trunk = boot (of a car); vacation = holiday; wait staff = waiter/waitress; zip code = post code*

ACCOMMODATION

Manor houses
Solares, casas nobres and *quintas* (often signposted as *turismo rural*) are old country houses, many still lived in by their owners, Information from local tourist offices.

Hotels and guest houses
By law, prices quoted for accommodation must include breakfast, although this admittedly does not always amount to much. There are various cat-

egories, ranging price-wise between $ 4,000 (two stars, low season) and $ 60,000 (five stars. high season). Guest houses *(pensão)* are mostly simple houses; prices: from $ 4,000 (two stars, low season) to $ 25,000 (four stars, high season). *Albergaria* and *residência* are bed and breakfast places: from $ 5,000 (three stars, low season) to $ 31,000 (five stars, high season). *Casas de hóspedes* are quite simple and accordingly very cheap guest houses. Estalagens are privately run hotels of varying standards.

Youth hostels
An international certificate of membership is required for your stay. Reservations and information from: *Albergues de Juventude, Rua Andrade Corvo 46, P-1050 Lisbon, Tel. 21/353 26 96*

Pousadas
Similar to the Spanish paradores, pousadas are state-owned hotels housed in selected and scenically beautiful places or in old castles, palaces, convents or manor houses. However, the standard of furnishing is not always as grand as the prices *(all Category 1)* would lead you to suppose. The most beautiful pousadas are men-

tioned under the relevant towns; also recommended are:

Pousada de Santa Maria de Bouro (32 rooms), Amares, Tel. 253/37 19 71, Fax 37 19 76, in an old Cistercian monastery

Pousada Dom Diniz (28 rooms), Vila Nova de Cerveira (near Valença), Tel. 251/79 56 01, Fax 79 56 04, in the town centre with a view of the town walls, some rooms with patio

Pousada da Ria (19 rooms), Murtosa (near Aveiro), Tel. 234/483 32, Fax 483 33, modern house by a lagoon

Pousada Rainha Santa Isabel (33 rooms), Estremoz, Tel. 268/33 20 75, Fax 33 20 79, in an old fortress and furnished in 12th/13th century style

Pousada de Nossa Senhora da Oliveira (16 rooms), Guimarães, Tel. 253/51 41 57, Fax 51 42 04, in an old manor house in the town centre.

BANKS & MONEY

The currency of the country is the Escudo (Esc), which is abbreviated to the dollar sign $. You can recognise cash machines by the sign MB (multibanco); they are to be found everywhere across the country. You can draw out up to $ 40,000 a day. The banks require a fee to exchange cash. All current credit cards are accepted in the larger hotels, at most filling stations and in many restaurants and shops. Bank opening times: Mon–Fri 8.30 am–3 pm, until 8 pm in some tourist centres.

CAMPING

"Wild" camping is not allowed.

There are more than 150 camping sites. List from : *Roteiro Campista, Apartado 3168, P-1304 Lisboa, Tel. 21/364 23 74, Fax 364 23 70*

CAR RENTAL

Branches of all major car rental firms can be found at airports, in large towns and cities and in tourist centres. For a car of the lower middle range you will have to pay between $ 8,200 and $ 12,300 a day plus VAT, fully comprehensive insurance and mileage charge; booking for a week is comparatively cheaper.

Some tourist agencies offer "fly and drive": the flight plus car rental at a particularly favourable all-in price. Those who have not booked in advance from home should compare prices locally; Portuguese rental firms are often considerably cheaper than their major international competitors, for example *Auto Jardim, Tel. 21/846 31 87 (Lisbon)* or *Tel. 289/58 97 15 (Albufeira)*.

Your own national driving licence suffices in Portugal; anyone renting a car must be at least 21 years of age and have held a licence for at least one year.

CUSTOMS

EU citizens travelling within the EU: All goods and items for personal use (including up to 800 cigarettes, 90 litres wine and 10 litres of spirits) are free from excise duty.

Travellers arriving from outside the EU: No duty is levied on personal effects including one camera or video camera, used portable radio or cassette player and items of sports equipment for personal use; in some instances an official receipt can be requested, which should then be produced when leaving the country. Duty free allowances include: up to 200 cigarettes, 50 cigars, 100 cigarillos or 250 grammes of tobacco, 2 litres of wine and other alcoholic drinks (of which 1 litre may be over 22%).

DOMESTIC FLIGHTS

As well as TAP, the Portugalia airline company with its small aircraft operates flights from Lisbon to Oporto, Braga, Bragança, Chaves, Vila Real, Viseu, Coimbra, Covilhã, Faro and Portimão.

DRIVING

International traffic regulations apply. Nevertheless be careful! The Portuguese driving style is somewhat unconventional – Portugal has the highest accident death rate in Europe. Speed limits: 50 km/h in built-up areas, 90 km/h on other roads and 120 km/h on highways (motorways). The blood alcohol limit is 0.5 per thousand (5 milligrams per millilitre), with the threat of imprisonment if over 1.25 per thousand (12.5 milligrams per millilitre). Children may not sit in the front seats. Warning: anyone caught using a phone while driving risks a heavy fine.

Filling stations are usually open from 7 am to midnight, 24 hours a day in large towns and on highways. Petrol is relatively expensive in Portugal. Lead-free (*sem chumbo*) is obtainable everywhere.

Breakdown assistance is provided by the *Automóvel Clube de*

Portugal ACP, emergency breakdown number for the north is *22/205 67 32*, and for the south *21/942 91 03*

EMBASSIES & CONSULATES

British Embassy
Rua de São Bernardo 33, 1249-082 Lisbon, Tel. 1/392 40 00, Fax 1/392 41 88

British Consulate
Av. da Boavista 3072, 4100-120 Oporto, Tel. 2/618 47 89, Fax 2/610 04 38

Canadian Embassy
Avenida da Liberdade 144/156, 4th Floor, 1250 Lisbon, Tel. 1/347 48 92, Fax 1/347 64 66

Canadian Consulate
P.O. Box 79, 8001 Faro, Tel. 89/80 37 57, Fax 89/88 08 88

US Embassy
Av. das Foráas Armadas, 1600 Lisbon, Tel. 1/727 33 00, Fax 1/727 91 09

EMERGENCIES

Police and ambulance
(countrywide): 112

Polícia de Segurança Pública
Tel. 21/346 61 41 or 347 47 30

HEALTH

For EU nationals form E111 is recognised in Portugal. Nevertheless, all visitors are advised to take out some form of short-term health insurance to avoid long waits. For nationals of non-EU countries private insurance cover is essential. Chemists (*far-*

mácia) can be found even in small towns (sign: a green cross, illuminated when open for all-night service). There are clinics and hospitals with permanent accident and emergency services in the larger towns; in rural areas the health centres *(centro de sáude)* are open from 8 am to 8 pm. *Red Cross in Lisbon: Tel. 21/301 77 77*

INFORMATION BEFORE YOU GO

Portuguese National Tourist Office In Great Britain
22–25a Sackville Street, 2nd Floor, London W1X 2LY, Tel. 020 7494 1441, Fax 020 7494 1868

In Canada
60 Bloor Street West, Suite 1005, Toronto ON M4W 3B8, Tel. 1 416 921-7376

In the United States
590 Fifth Avenue, 4th Floor, New York 10036-4704, Tel. 1 212 354-4403

88 Kearny Street, Suite 1770, San Francisco, CA 941 08, Tel. 1 415 391-7080

1900 L Street, Suite 310, Washington DC 20036, Tel. 1 202 331–8222

INFORMATION IN PORTUGAL

The *Turismo* offices have varying opening times, many are open daily from 9.30 am to 7 pm during the season, until 5 pm in the winter, often with a lunch break. Freephone number for tourist information 9 am–midnight: *Tel. 2800 29 62 96*

MEDIA

Most hotel rooms have television. Satellite programmes are broadcast in Portuguese, English, German and French.

In the larger towns and cities and in many holiday areas, British and American newspapers and magazines are usually available on the day of publication.

Surfers of the internet will enjoy themselves in Portugal: *Ciber Chiado, Espaço Ágora* and *Planet Megastore* are Lisbon's best-known internet cafés; this service is also being increasingly offered in other tourist centres.

NUDISM & GOING TOPLESS

Nudism is prohibited in Catholic Portugal, going topless is tolerated on most beaches. There are official nude beaches to the south of Lisbon on the Praia da Belavista and near Meco.

OPENING HOURS

Shops open daily (except Sunday) from 9 am–1 pm and 3–6 pm; many tobacconists, food shops and shopping centres also open on Sundays and until late in the evening.

PASSPORTS & VISAS

To enter Portugal British, US and Canadian citizens only need a valid passport. Visas are not required for visits up to 90 days.

By car
To enter Portugal by car (there are 17 border crossing points) you will need a valid driving licence (your national one is suf-

ficient), vehicle registration documents and an International Green Card.

With animals

For domestic animals a current certificate of health from a qualified veterinary surgeon, (giving details of the background and pedigree and health of the animal), duly translated into Portuguese. A certificate of inoculation against rabies must date back at least 30 days but no longer than one year and contain the date of the inoculation and show the type of vaccine used. Before leaving Portugal both certificates should be witnessed by the Portuguese consulate.

PHOTOGRAPHY

Allowed everywhere unless expressly forbidden (e.g. in museums and churches). Films and other photographic materials are very expensive in Portugal, so it is better to take them with you. For the most part light conditions are such that photosensitive film is not necessary.

POST

Post office opening times

Mon–Fri 8.30 am–12.30 pm and 2.30–6 pm. From 9 am–8 pm on the Praça do Comércio and the Praça dos Restauradores in Lisbon and also at the airport.

Postage

Cards and letters to EU countries cost $ 95, to other European countries $ 100. As well as in post offices, stamps can be purchased in all shops displaying a red horse or a white circle on a green background (mainly stationers and tobacconists). Post boxes are red, except those for "correio azul" (express post) which are blue.

PUBLIC TRANSPORT

Rail

The most modern stretch of line in Portugal is the IC link between Oporto and Lisbon. Single fare 1st class $ 5,150, 2nd class $ 3,150. All other rail links in Portugal are not very comfortable by European standards but they are punctual. A 7-day tourist card costs $ 18,000 (1st class), a 14-day card $ 30,000, a 21-day card $ 42,000. There are nostalgic rides to be had in northern Portugal on the Tâmego stretch between Livração and Arco de Baúlhe. Old steam locomotives pull special coaches through extremely varying countryside.

Buses, trams and underground

Bus travel is cheap, comfortable and well organised. Even outlying places are served by a dense network of routes. Fares average about $ 1,540 per 100 kilometres.

In Lisbon you pay $ 450 for the *Aero Bus* (every 20 minutes) from the airport into the city. The ticket is then valid for the rest of that day on all forms of public transport in the city.

A journey on the underground in Lisbon costs $ 100, a 10-journey ticket is $ 800. With the *Lisboa Card* you can travel free and for unlimited distances on buses, the underground, trams and lifts in Lisbon, together with free admission to 26 museums and other places of interest. The card costs $ 1,900 for 24 hours, $ 3,100 for 48 hours and $ 4,000 for 72 hours.

It can be bought at *Rua Jardim do Regedor 50* among other places,

Boat trips

Tejo: April to October all day excursions, in the high season also evening cruises with dinner on board. Departure: Lisbon, Terreiro do Paço.

Douro: Tuesday to Sunday excursions from the Cais da Ribeira in Oporto. Evening trips with candle light dinner in high summer.

Guadiana: day tour on the border river in the Algarve from Vila Real to Alcoutim.

Taxis

Taxis are relatively cheap in Portugal. From 10 pm to 6 am there is a 20 per cent surcharge.

There is a brochure which contains contact addresses for all kinds of sports in which tourists can participate in Portugal. Called "Sports and Activities", it can be obtained free of charge from the Portuguese tourist office and all other tourist offices.

In the larger towns post offices offer telex and fax facilities, as do most hotels.

Local calls cost $ 17.50 per minute. Overseas calls can be made from any public telephone. For this you will need $ 50 coins. More practical and more and more common is the telephone card costing $ 875 or $ 2,100. A one-minute call to Britain costs about $ 210 during the day, $ 150 after 8 pm.

Dialling codes to Portugal:
From the UK 00 351
From the United States and Canada 011 351
Dialling codes from Portugal:
To the UK 00 44
To the USA and Canada 061

Portugal observes Greenwich Mean Time (GMT) also known as Western European Time, which is five hours ahead of US Eastern Standard Time and eight hours ahead of Pacific Time. Clocks go forward one hour at the end of March and back one hour at the end of October.

A service charge is included in the bill in hotels and restaurants. Nevertheless, a tip of between 5 and 15 per cent is always gratefully accepted. Room-maids, taxi drivers, porters and shoeshine boys all expect a small tip.

The current is 220 volts with continental two-pin plugs. British and American/Canadian plugs require an adaptor.

1 cm	0.39 inch
1 m	1.09 yd (3.28 ft)
1 km	0.62 miles
1 sq m	1.20 sq yds
1 ha	2.47 acres
1 sq km	0.39 sq miles
1 g	0.035 ounces
1 kg	2.21 pounds
1 British ton	1016 kg
1 US ton	907 kg

1 litre is equivalent to 0.22 Imperial gallons and 0.26 US gallons

WHEN TO GO

The best times to go to Portugal are spring (mid-March to early June) and autumn (September to end of October). The high season is from 1 May to 30 September. The bathing season lasts from May to September in the north and almost the whole year in the south.

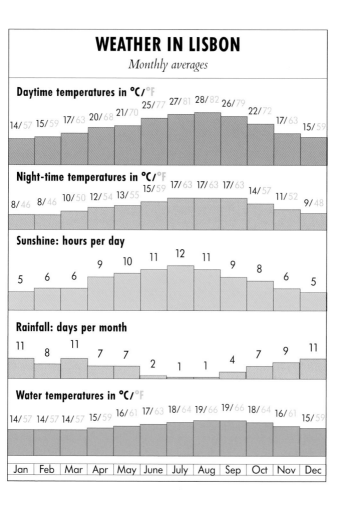

WEATHER IN LISBON
Monthly averages

Daytime temperatures in °C/°F

14/57 15/59 17/63 20/68 21/70 25/77 27/81 28/82 26/79 22/72 17/63 15/59

Night-time temperatures in °C/°F

8/46 8/46 10/50 12/54 13/55 15/59 17/63 17/63 17/63 14/57 11/52 9/48

Sunshine: hours per day

5 6 6 9 10 11 12 11 9 8 6 5

Rainfall: days per month

11 8 11 7 7 2 1 1 4 7 9 11

Water temperatures in °C/°F

14/57 14/57 14/57 15/59 16/61 17/63 18/64 19/66 19/66 18/64 16/61 15/59

| Jan | Feb | Mar | Apr | May | June | July | Aug | Sep | Oct | Nov | Dec |

Do's and don'ts

Even in Portugal there are occasional crimes involving tourists and things which are best avoided

Most Portuguese are basically honest people and would not dream of "taking tourists for a ride". As a result there are few crimes against tourists and only a few cases of "rip-offs". The fact that a sea trip with evening meal will not be cheap should be obvious; equally, a candlelit dinner with fado music in Lisbon's Old Town will make a hole in the holiday budget (from $ 6,150 per person), but you may be lucky and have not only an excellent chef but also a really good lady vocalist.

Certainly you should keep your eyes open in the main tourist centres: there are pickpockets everywhere in the world, including Portugal. "Touts", as they are known in the bazaars of the Near East, only pester tourists in particular holiday resorts. And taxi drivers who "forget" to cancel their meters should be asked to do this at the start of the journey.

A peck on the cheek here, a peck on the cheek there

Bestowing *beijinhos* (little kisses) is an art you will soon learn. Even though it seems as though in Portugal everybody kisses everybody else there is a correct form of etiquette: 1. Never greet a stranger with a kiss. 2. Kiss only once (twice in rural areas), and only on the right cheek. 3. A delicate brush against the cheek will suffice. 4. Avoid any other form of contact.

Quarteira

It lies 24 km west of Faro airport and is said to be the ugliest town in the whole of Portugal. This is probably why travel agents and property dealers avoid the flats here like the plague. The new part of town consists of a wide Avenida and some repulsive high-rise buildings: frighteningly devoid of people in winter and hopelessly deserted in summer, this town is definitely not a "must"!

Underestimating the sun and the sea

In northern Portugal take warm clothing and rainwear with you at all times of the year. When bathing or indulging in water sports do not underestimate the wild Atlantic coast! Always pay due regard to warning flags: a green one means bathing is safe, red means danger and swimming is prohibited. Moreover, on no account fail to protect yourself against the sun!

Road Atlas of Portugal

*Please refer to back cover for an overview
of this Road Atlas*

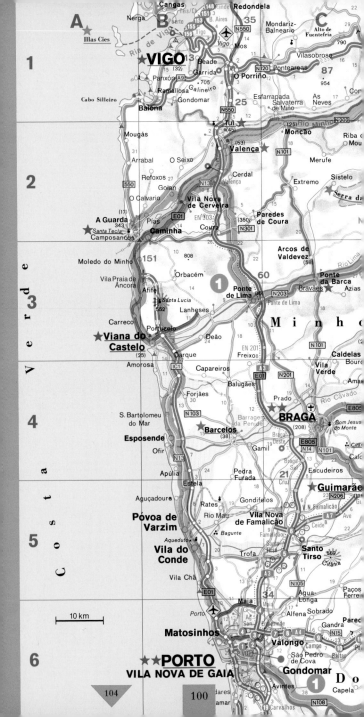

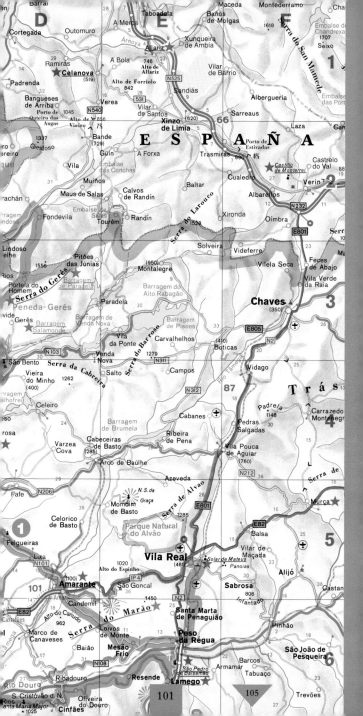

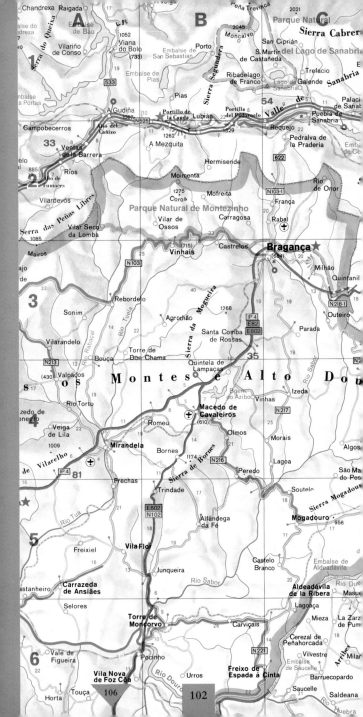

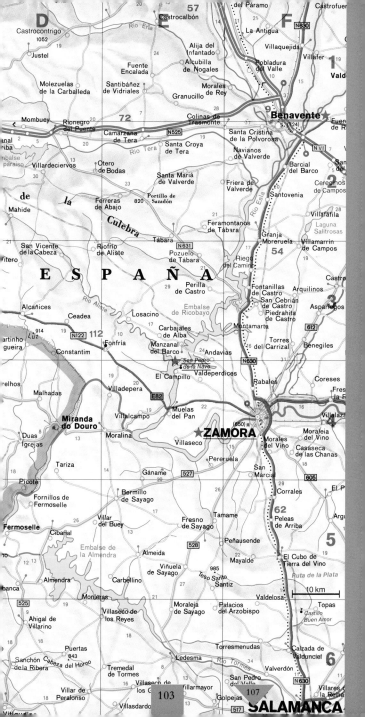

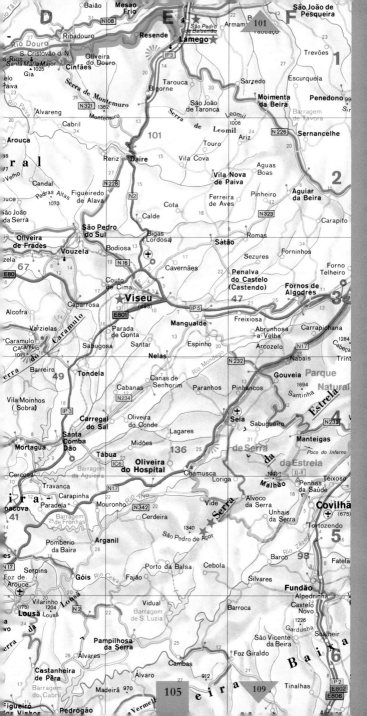

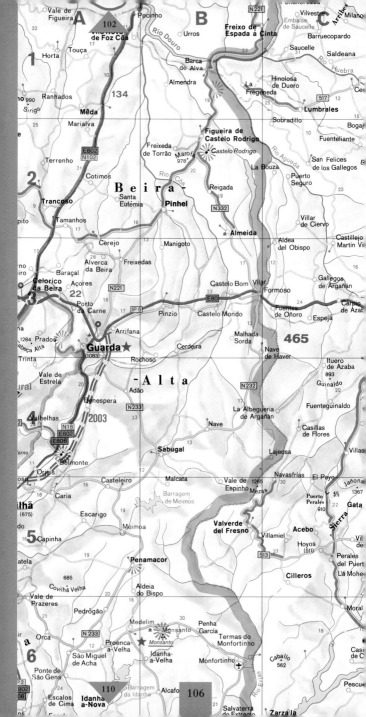

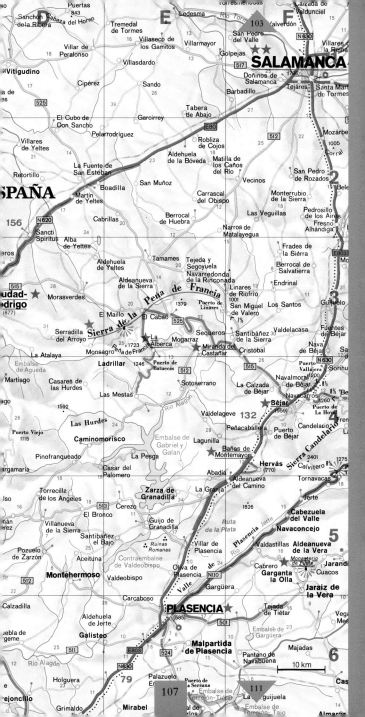

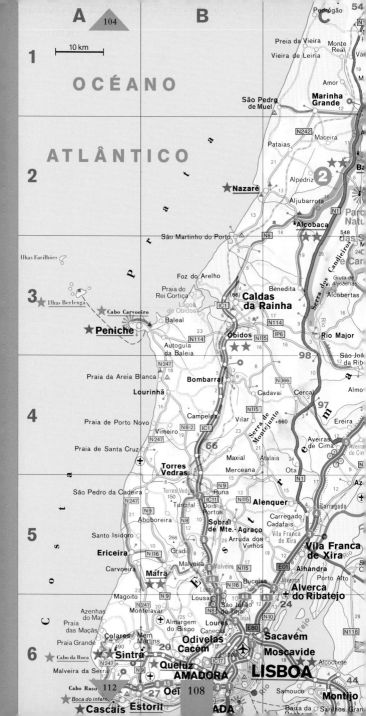

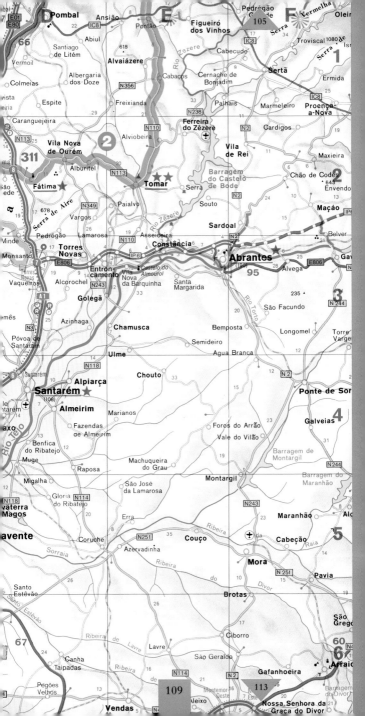

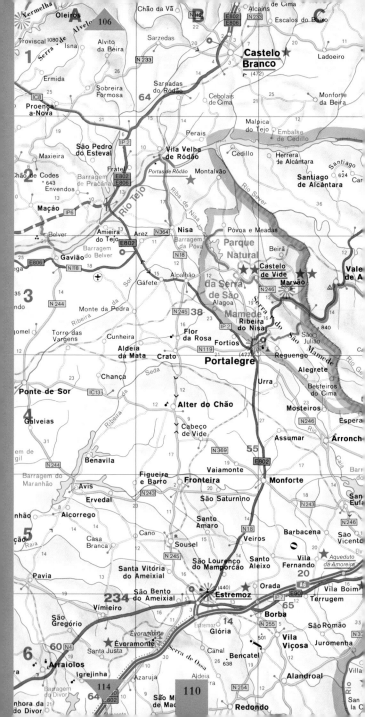

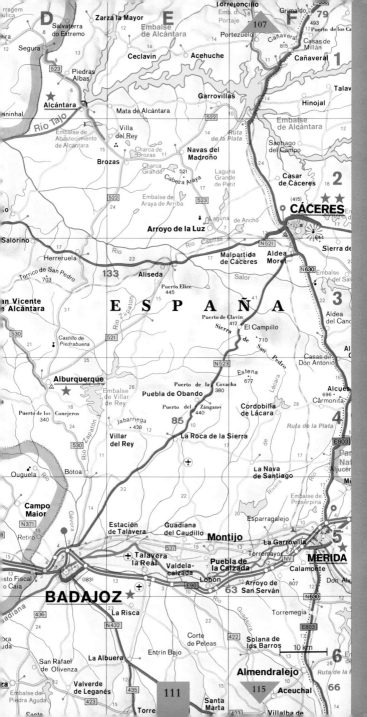

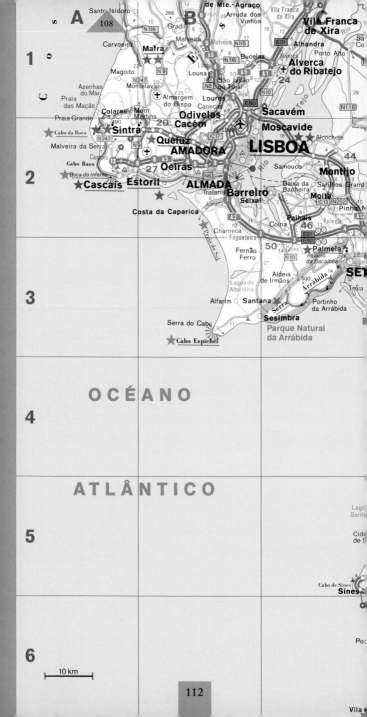

Santo Isidoro
266
de Mte.-Agraço
Arruda dos
Vinhos
26
Vila Franca
de Xira
Gradil
10
Vila Franca
de Xira
Carvoeira
N116
Malveira
Malveira
17
19
E01
12
Alhandra
Mafra
A8
8
Bucelas
N116
A9
Porto Alto
Alverca
Alverca
Magoito
N9
Louça
24
do Ribatejo
Azenhas
do Mar
N247
Montelavar
São Julião
do Tojal
N8
12
Tojal
N10
29
Almargem
do Bispo
Loures
E80
N118
Praia
das Maças
Canecas
Colares
Mem
Martins
Odivelas
16
Sacavém
Praia Grande
490
Cacém
Estádio
★Cabo da Roca
Sintra
20
IC17
18
Moscavide
Alcochete
N247
N9
Queluz
44
Malveira da Serra
AMADORA
LISBOA
Cabo Raso
12
A5
Oelras
N6
Samouco
Montijo
Boca do Inferno
27
Baixa da
Banheira
Sarilhos Grand
2
★**Cascais**
Estoril
12
ALMADA
46
Moita
IC13 N252
Trafaria
Barreiro
Pinhal N
Almada
Seixal
A12
Costa da Caparica
A2
Coina
Palmela
10
Charneca
13
Palmela
Fogueteiro
Coina
E01
E90
Fernão
Ferro
50
14
Coina
Palmela
Palmela
N10
Palácio
da Bacalhoa
Lagoa de
Albufeira
Aldeia
de Irmãos
500
14
SE
Arrábida
Alfarim
Santana
Serra
Tróia
3
Portinho
da Arrábida
Serra do Cabo
11
Sesimbra
★**Cabo Espichel**
Parque Natural
da Arrábida

OCÉANO

4

ATLÂNTICO

Lago
Sante

Cida
de S

5

Cabo de Sines
Sines

Po

6

10 km

Vila

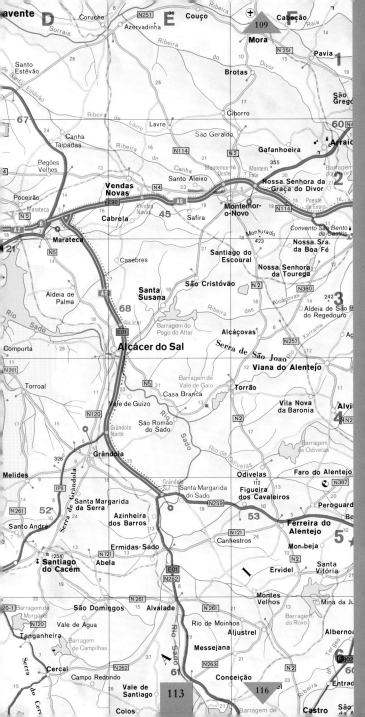

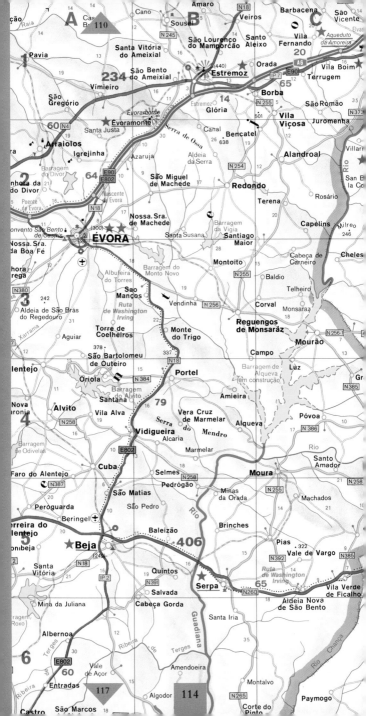

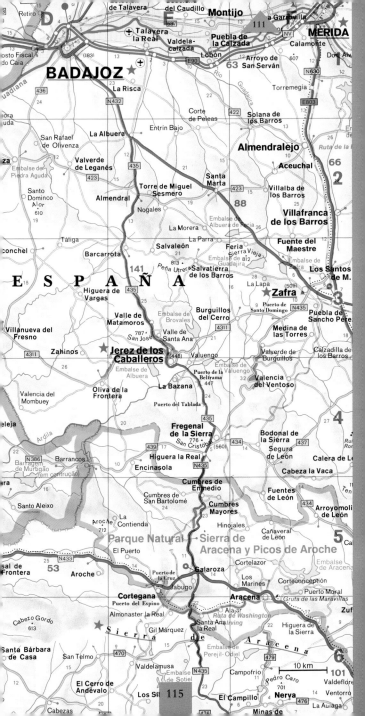

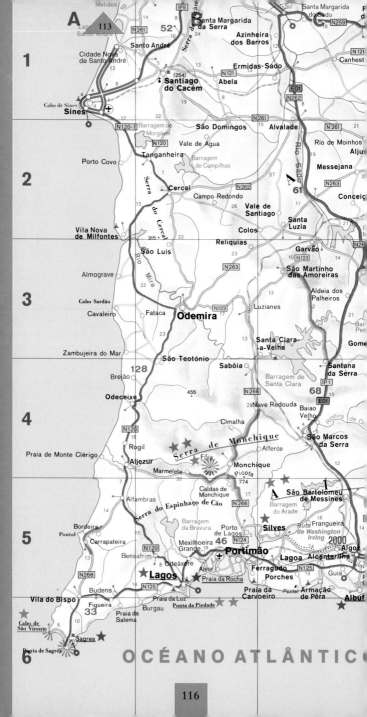

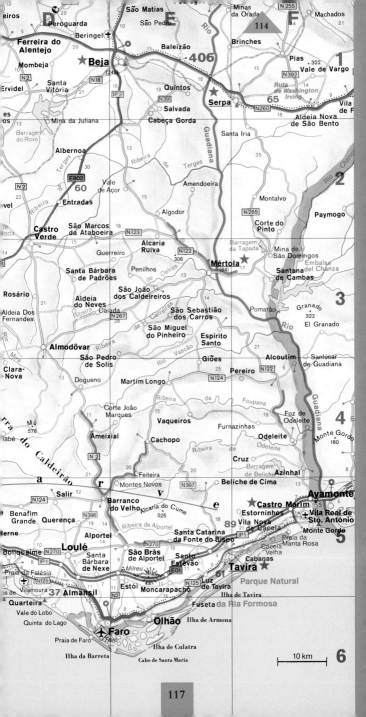

ROAD ATLAS LEGEND

le Mans-Est **4**	Autobahn mit Anschlußstelle / Motorway with junction
Datum, Date	Autobahn in Bau / Motorway under construction
Datum, Date	Autobahn in Planung / Motorway projected
®	Raststätte mit Übernachtungsmöglichkeit / Roadside restaurant and hotel
®	Raststätte ohne Übernachtungsmöglichkeit / Roadside restaurant
®	Erfrischungsstelle, Kiosk / Snackbar, kiosk
®	Tankstelle / Filling-station
	Autobahnähnliche Schnellstraße mit Anschlußstelle / Dual carriage-way with motorway characteristics with junction
	Straße mit zwei getrennten Fahrbahnen / Dual carriage-way
	Durchgangsstraße / Thoroughfare
	Wichtige Hauptstraße / Important main road
	Hauptstraße / Main road
	Sonstige Straße / Other road
	Fernverkehrsbahn / Main line railway
	Bergbahn / Mountain railway
	Autotransport per Bahn / Transport of cars by railway
	Autofähre / Car ferry
	Schiffahrtslinie / Shipping route
	Landschaftlich besonders schöne Strecke / Route with beautiful scenery
Routes des Crêtes	Touristenstraße / Tourist route
	Straße gegen Gebühr befahrbar / Toll road
X — X — X	Straße für Kraftfahrzeuge gesperrt / Road closed to motor traffic
⊢⊢⊢⊢⊢⊢	Zeitlich geregelter Verkehr / Temporal regulated traffic
← 15% →	Bedeutende Steigungen / Important gradients

Kultur
Culture

★★ **PARIS** ★★ *la Alhambra*	Eine Reise wert / Worth a journey
★ **TRENTO** ★ *Comburg*	Lohnt einen Umweg / Worth a detour

Landschaft
Landscape

★★ **Rodos** ★★ *Fingal's cave*	Eine Reise wert / Worth a journey
★ **Korab** ★ *Jaskinia raj*	Lohnt einen Umweg / Worth a detour
☀ ⩔	Besonders schöner Ausblick / Important panoramic view
	Nationalpark, Naturpark / National park, nature park
	Sperrgebiet / Prohibited area
4807 ▲	Bergspitze mit Höhenangabe in Metern / Mountain summit with height in metres
(630)	Ortshöhe / Elevation
⋅	Kirche / Church
⋅	Kirchenruine / Church ruin
⋅	Kloster / Monastery
⋅	Klosterruine / Monastery ruin
⋅	Schloß, Burg / Palace, castle
⋅	Schloß-, Burgruine / Palace ruin, castle ruin
⋅	Denkmal / Monument
/	Wasserfall / Waterfall
⋒	Höhle / Cave
∴	Ruinenstätte / Ruins
⋅	Sonstiges Objekt / Other object
△	Jugendherberge / Youth hostel
🏖 🏄	Badestrand · Surfen / Bathing beach · Surfing
🤿 🎣	Tauchen · Fischen / Diving · Fishing
✈	Verkehrsflughafen / Airport
⊕	Flugplatz / Airfield

20 km

118

INDEX

This index lists all the main places and sights mentioned in this guide. Numbers in bold indicate a main entry, italics a photograph.

What do you get for your money?

 The unit of currency is the escudo. Bank notes are in denominations of 500, 1000, 2,000, 5,000 and 10,000 escudos. The abbreviation for escudo is a dollar sign.

The best rates of exchange can usually be obtained in Portugal, although in the case of travellers' cheques the commission charged may negate any such benefit.

A small coffee, a bica, costs $ 100 to 250, a coffee with milk, known as a galão, from $ 160, an orange juice from $ 200, a freshly pulled beer – depending on the pub – from $ 150 and a bottle of wine in a bar from $ 500: a piece of cake costs between $ 100 and $ 250, a bread roll with fish or meat from $ 100. Anyone thinking of spending an evening in a fado establishment should expect to have to pay at least $ 4,500 a head for entry and drinks. The theatre (from $ 3,000), the opera and ballet (from $ 2,000) and the cinema ($ 800, Mondays $ 500), on the other hand, are comparatively cheap. The admission charges for museums in Portugal vary according to the season. While in winter many museums charge only $ 250 this can treble in summer. Tickets for some bull fights cost from $ 3,500.

US $	Escudo	£	Escudo	Can $	Escudo
1	214	1	338	1	145
2	428	2	676	2	290
3	642	3	1,014	3	435
4	856	4	1,352	4	580
5	1,070	5	1,690	5	725
10	2,140	10	3,380	10	1,450
15	3,210	15	5,070	15	2,175
20	4,280	20	6,760	20	2,900
25	5,350	25	8,450	25	3,625
30	6,420	30	10,140	30	4,350
40	8,560	40	13,520	40	5,800
50	10,700	50	16,900	50	7,250
60	12,840	60	20,280	60	8,700
70	14,980	70	23,660	70	10,150
80	17,120	80	27,040	80	11,600
90	19,260	90	30,420	90	13,050
100	21,400	100	33,800	100	14,500
200	42,800	200	67,600	200	29,000
300	64,200	300	101,400	300	43,500
400	85,600	400	135,200	400	58,000
500	107,000	500	169,000	500	72,500
750	160,500	750	253,500	750	108,750
1,000	214,000	1,000	338,000	1,000	145,000

These exchange rates are for guidance only and are correct at May 2000. You are advised to check with a bank or tourist office before travelling.